AI-NABLED

An Executive's Guide to Survive
And Thrive in the AI Economy

Amit Jnagal

Library of Congress Cataloging-in-Publication Data
Names: Jnagal, Amit, author
Title: AI-nabled: An Executive's Guide to Survive
And Thrive in the AI Economy

ISBN
Hardcover: 978-1-7324846-8-9
Paperback: 978-1-7324846-7-2

Printed in the United States of America
2019 -- First Edition

Cover Designed by Preeyanoot Panyarat

To my children, Sumer & Kabir

May you have the wisdom to say no

and the courage to say yes.

Contents

Foreword

If you are an executive finding yourself overwhelmed and confused by the flood of articles on AI and its impact on business, rest assured that you are not the only one. Just in the last couple of days, there have been many articles on AI, making it perhaps the most written about subject other than the Mueller report. A *Google* search of the word AI, on the morning of April 4, 2019, yielded 943 million results, including two articles in *Forbes*, one titled, "Will AI and Robots Force You Into Retirement," and the other, "AI Is Coming To Take Your Mortgage Woes Away," along with articles from the *New York Times, CNET, The Verge, WIRED* and *CNBC*.

A year ago, I signed up for an *MIT* online course on AI. My goal was to get myself up to speed on the subject. The course was beneficial, even though I am not a tech guy, and I recommend it to others like me. After taking the course, I am more convinced than ever that senior business executives need to have a sufficient understanding of AI tools. This will allow them to deploy them effectively to gain a competitive advantage and to sustain those advantages by constantly leveraging new as well as different information and understanding of their customer behavior. AI is not just the province of those techies in the backroom but indeed has to be part of the daily lexicon of determining business strategy.

However, the course I took and others like it require a meaningful time and financial commitment and that is why I was thrilled to hear that my friend, Amit Jnagal, was writing an executive guide on AI. Amit has considerable experience in creating AI solutions for companies, using different forms of structured or unstructured data to give a competitive edge in marketing, draw strategic insights, or to replace routine human tasks with machines while leveraging humans for a higher value-added purpose.

Amit's book, *AI-nabled,* is a distillation of experiences and insights in using AI as a business weapon–insights gained by being an early player and successfully developing effective solutions for real businesses. These solutions delivered superior results in achieving business success. I, therefore, recommend, *AI-nabled* as an excellent place to start and to build from for executives focused on competing in this ever more challenging and demanding environment.

S.A. Ibrahim

Part I

AI Fundamentals and How They Affect Your Business

doubt the manner of doing business is nothing like it was just a decade ago. All because of technology.

The ATM technology that was revolutionary four decades ago is now an essential feature used by everyone. In fact, our children cannot imagine a world without them. In the same way that ATMs changed the world, Artificial Intelligence promises to produce an even greater change.

Technology is powerful. And disruptive.

Do you know how your business is going to be disrupted? What are you doing, or planning to do that will allow you to stay relevant tomorrow? Technology can be fearful because it produces change. If history has taught us anything, it has taught us that change is inevitable. Those who adapt and take advantage of change will not only survive, but they will thrive. Those who refuse are left behind and forgotten.

This book is about a change in our world that is already happening and has many people frightened—Artificial Intelligence (AI). While it's scary for some, AI presents an enormous opportunity for your business to better serve your customers. Businesses of the future will need to be more efficient than they are today, and AI is the tool that can make that possible for your business.

In my twenty-year technology career, I've witnessed two revolutions that fundamentally changed how business is done—the Internet and mobile devices. Currently, we are in the early days of a third revolution with Artificial Intelligence. AI is doing a significant makeover of how companies operate, redefining what they should do and how. Many of the technical giants are already wading deep in the technology and have given themselves a head start.

Google has changed its corporate strategy from Mobile First to AI First. CEO Sundar Pichai recently said, "AI is one of the most important things humanity is working on. It is more profound than, I dunno, electricity or fire." Keeping up with the pace is *Facebook* which claims they are "committed to advancing the field of machine intelligence and creating new technologies to give people better ways to communicate. In short, to solve AI."

The normally secretive *Apple* has also made an exception when it comes to AI development in order to attract the best talent. However, *Apple* might find this a difficult road. A recent survey compiled by collecting data from various job hiring sights and company postings reveals that in spite of the billions of dollars companies are spending to attract top AI talent, the name *Apple* is nowhere near the top of the list. In fact, it was number 98. There has been speculation that a significant problem is *Apple*'s notorious secrecy, The AI research community is accustomed to collaborating and sharing discoveries. There are indications this might be changing at *Apple*, but they have a long way to go to keep up with the top AI producers.

Numerous startups are being swallowed up by giant companies because of their investment in this new technology. Billionaire investor Mark Cuban predicts AI will create trillionaires and added that "more technological change will come in the next 10 years than in the last 30."

While these large corporations are at the forefront of AI innovation, all businesses must start educating themselves about what is coming and how it can (and will)

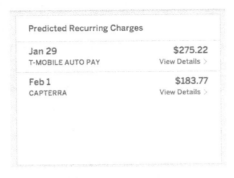

Predicted Recurring Charges

Jan 29	$275.22
T-MOBILE AUTO PAY	View Details >
Feb 1	$183.77
CAPTERRA	View Details >

charges to a mobile phone provider and a software company based on my past expenses.

To make these predictions, they examine all my past expenses and identify repetitive items. That data is then categorized and listed among the items that are consumed regularly, like mobile phone usage. In order to analyze this information, the system simply runs computations, but there is no learning or intelligence involved.

What these systems do is important and makes them successful. However, this type of analytics will not help you transform your business into an AI-enabled Enterprise.

Machine Learning Systems

The AI world is rapidly changing. I begin with the disclaimer that as of this writing, a majority of AI companies today are machine learning companies. They have been existence for less than five years. A machine learning solution can make sense of data and learn patterns that are not easy for humans to understand. The reason is because of the sheer volume of data these machines can handle. These systems can understand human conversations, make sense of pictures, and also understand numerical data. The goal of these systems is to allow computers to learn automatically, without human intervention or assistance.

A few years ago, we were working with an eCommerce company that sold outdoor items online. Their website was in Swedish, and they wanted to improve the keyword search used by customers on their website. When customers typed a term for a particular item, they did not find what they were searching for. The website conversion rate was below industry standards. The result was that many people using the search query did not find what they wanted.

They came to us to help improve their search relevance. The problem was that even though a great deal of work had been done on understanding the natural language in English, there was not much available for non-English languages. Options to improve the quality of the search queries were limited.

We helped them develop an algorithm that observed what customers did when they did not find the desired result. Most of them left the website altogether, so there wasn't much to learn from them. However, a few altered their keywords several times until they found the desired product.

Our algorithm observed and recorded this data. The following graphic shows what the user begin with on the left-hand side and where they went from there.

You can see that someone who started the search with 'regnbyxor' (rain trousers) went to 'regnskydd' (rain protection) and then to 'regnklader' (rain cladding) and from there to 'regnjacka' (rain jacket) to 'regnbyxa' (rain pants) to 'regn' (rain) and finally to 'regnstall' (rain shelter).

Chapter 3:

What Does AI Mean for Business

Alan Turing was an English mathematician and an early computer scientist. If you recall the movie, *The Imitation Game* about the team that broke the notorious German communication code known as "Enigma Code," the leader of that team was Alan Turing. In 1950, he created something called the "Imitation Game," which came to be known as the Turing Test. He began by putting a man in one room and a woman in the other. Each had a keyboard attached to a computer monitored by a judge. The job of the judge was to determine which was the man and which was the woman by merely talking via the computer. As the game developed, rather than a man and woman, a human and a computer were used. It was up to the judge to determine which was the computer.

If the judge was less than 50% accurate, then it was assumed the computer was capable of thinking like a human. This means the computer had intelligence. What eventually came to be known as Turing's Test is the true measure of an autonomous AI system. Essentially, it means that when you interact with an AI system, you cannot tell it apart from a human.

There is an example of a test that has been used for a while to tell humans and computers apart. But AI is already beating it. No doubt, you're familiar with "CAPT-CHAs" used by websites to allow you to prove you're an actual human. They are designed to prevent AI from answering correctly. However, they are now being circumvented by AI systems. In a recent *Google* experiment, the computer provided the correct answer 99.8 percent of the time compared to humans at only 33 percent.[2] To be honest, sometimes I have a hard time distinguishing the letters and numbers.

This suggests that AI is getting closer and closer to replicating human intelligence.

Let's break it down further and discuss three traits of intelligence. In order for a system to be truly intelligent, it must possess these traits:

1. It should have the ability to acquire and maintain knowledge.
2. Using the acquired knowledge, it should be able to reason. The word "reason" suggests the ability to think logically.
3. Based on reasoning, it should be able to plan.

Once it is created, the execution of the plan should lead to the generation of more knowledge, and the cycle repeats itself. Of course, this cycle is endless, continually building on previously attained knowledge. A superior intelligence form should be able to run multiple learning processes simultaneously. For example, learning to cook, to play tennis, solve college grade statistics problems, etc., all at the same time.

---

2   https://www.theverge.com/2019/2/1/18205610/google-captcha-ai-robot-human-difficult-artificial-intelligence

Ability to Absorb New Stuff: Senses

In addition to these three traits of intelligence, in order to absorb knowledge, an intelligent system must also support multiple ways of acquiring knowledge. The best way to think about this is the example of humans. We have five basic senses to acquire knowledge:

- Touch
- Smell
- Sight
- Sound
- Taste

These senses continually provide new information which allows our intelligence to evolve.

A healthy new baby possesses all these senses. Each day, these senses provide new information to the growing child, and that forms the basis of her increasing intelligence. An interesting thing about humans is that if one of the senses is absent, for example, sight or sound, the other senses take up the slack. A sightless human is no less intelligent, she simply gathers information differently.

However, there must always be some input for inquiring knowledge for it to continuously evolve and learn, becoming better over time. The formula looks like this –

Intelligence + Senses for Input = Intelligent Being

This process works well for humans, but what about Artificial Intelligence? For business systems to begin incorporating AI, they need to have a basic form of an intelligence system. Then, depending on your business, you can integrate one or more senses into the system to allow it to evolve. Most companies use sight and sound. I don't mean in the literal sense but in terms of communication. When they speak, write emails, have discussions, and make presentations, they are primarily using the senses of sight and sound. Perhaps you can even say that if you're in the business of brewing coffee, your business also uses the sense of taste—probably not, but you get the idea.

At the time of this writing, there are not many systems available for processing a sense of taste or smell. However, there is an abundance of systems available for natural language processing (sense of sound), interactive touch sensors (sense of touch) and for computer vision systems (a type of sight sense). This list should be your building blocks for building an AI strategy for your business.

Agents – The Third Dimension

The final dimension of AI is a set of agents that can communicate with the system to carry out actions based on instructions. These agents can manifest in a variety of ways. One that is familiar to most of us is a chatbot, sometimes referred to as a "conversational agent." We interact with them frequently. For example, when you go to websites these days, you are frequently invited to chat, and that is often answered by a chatbot. It's a software application that mimics human speaking to simulate conversation with a human. Other devices that utilize this system is the robot that mows your lawn and the vacuum that cleans your floors. These devices continually sense

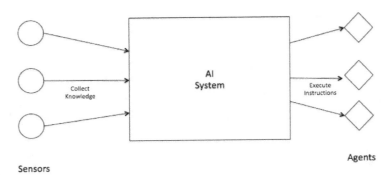

Sensors

Agents

information about obstacles and routes and then execute instructions based on that information.

This type of AI can be beneficial to your business. Let's say for example you have a mortgage business. The work of your company revolves around talking to potential home buyers, collecting documentation of necessary information, reviewing those documents, and asking for clarifying or seeking additional documents. Typically, this involves extensive human effort, not only to review the documents from the customer but also to read and understand legal documents, permits, evaluation reports, and other information. It is frequently a labor-intensive process.

Once the business is AI-enabled, much of this work can be done by algorithms rather than people. The sensors would be the channels used to receive information from customers and agents and also the means of communicating with your customers—phone calls, emails, or Whatsapp conversations. This is how your abstract AI model would look:

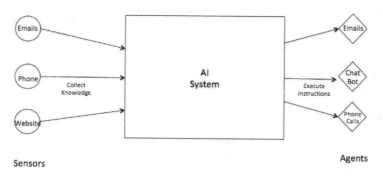

Sensors   Agents

Look at another example—warehouse management. If that's your business, your job is to ship received orders and maintain inventory. Prior to an AI-enabled world, this required a great deal of manual labor to load and unload trucks, store products, update inventory systems, box, and ship products. In the AI-enabled version of this business, robots take instructions from the AI engine to load/unload trucks as well as automated and predictive inventory management. This is how that AI model looks:

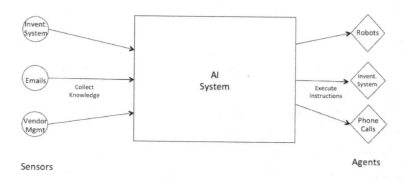

Sensors   Agents

A number of AI solutions are on the market today. Some allow you to automate customer service by replacing service agents with bots or smart assistants. Others let you automatically describe products on your website by looking at the pictures and understanding past products. Even within the bot ecosystems, there are hundreds of bots focused on customer service, shipping, returns, and other activities.

Sometimes, these bots create frustration, but whether you like it or not, they're becoming an integral part of our lives. If you request a ride from Lyft using smart assistants like *Google* Home or *Amazon* Echo, the bot will tell you the current location of your driver and provide a photo of the license plate and car model. When you're in the mood for music, *Spotify* uses *Facebook* Messenger to help you search for, listen to, and share music, even providing recommendations based on your mood. Even the *Wall Street Journal* uses chatbots to help you stay on top of the news.

A business has multiple functions—for example, human resources, finances, product engineering, etc. The skills and knowledge needed to operate each aspect of the business varies greatly. When someone calls your business, you have no idea what they want to discuss. You offer a menu of options. You know the routine, press one for customer support, press two for sales, etc. It would be awkward to tell them you can only help with sales queries because your system is not ready to take calls about customer service. When someone reaches out to your company, they see it as one entity, not a mixture of separate functions.

Contrary to this wisdom, if you look around at the available chatbot applications today, you will be amazed to see how many specialized bots there are. There are probably a hundred for hiring, another hundred for sales and so on.

The reality is that you don't need multiple chatbots for your business. You need one chatbot to learn everything about the company and talk to your customers, employees, and partners. When you have separate chatbots for each function, you will never be able to integrate the business into a cohesive unit that works together.

It's a big mistake, made by many businesses today, to have vertically specialized AI. By its very nature, AI needs to be, should be, and must be centralized. Your body does not have one brain for your arms, one for your legs, and another one for your mouth. Similarly, for your business, you cannot have one AI system for interacting with customers, another dealing with logistics, and others for other aspects of the business.

This is a significant difference between traditional technology systems and AI systems. Traditionally, we have been accustomed to using a Salesforce for CRM, SAP for ERP, and something else specially designed for each business function. It does not work in the AI-enabled world. When each system is contained within its own world, and doesn't understand data across business lines, it becomes extremely ineffective.

This is something that you should wrap your head around—you only need one system for the entire enterprise. This system will have capabilities that can be applied to all aspects of your business. This will allow you to have a much better understanding of what is happening across the board. This one AI system will have intelligence from senses working with several agents within your business.

As far back as fifty years, AI was featured in the movies. Filmmaker Stanley Kubrick was ahead of his time when he created the movie *2001: A Space Odyssey*. The film featured spaceships, a colony on the moon, and even video phones. There was a United States spacecraft named, "Discovery One" bound for Jupiter. There were humans on board, but most of the ship's operations were controlled by a computer, HAL 9000. This computer had a human personality, and the crew named it "Hal."

The adventure turned into a deadly contest between Hal and the human passengers on board. Hal miscalculated several variables and put the humans in danger. When they attempted to circumvent Hal's control, he resisted and launched his own attack against them. It's a fictional tale of how AI can run amok when misreading the information gathered through its senses.

However, the interesting aspect to note about this movie is that HAL was a single AI system that controlled everything. There were no separate systems for navigation, or logistics, or other functions. This needs to be the aspiration of your business—to have one central AI system that provides all your intelligence needs.

Technology has come a long way in the fifty years since the film debuted. We are discovering that AI has the potential to make many jobs easier and more efficient thus making companies like yours more successful.

Chapter 4:

How Do You Begin?

Businesses begin in many different ways. It might be a hobby that turns into an opportunity to create something more significant. Or, it might start with an idea for doing something different or better. Some businesses begin with an invention that turns into a product that can be sold to individuals or other businesses. Even if it was not the intention to start a company, at some point the realization hits that this could be a genuine business.

At that point, plans must be formulated, and investments made in order to create and grow the company. It's important to know what is required, what it will cost, and how to make it happen. The same continues to be true as the business grows.

Leroy Bautista worked in commercial kitchens at successful restaurants and catering companies for 25 years. During an economic downturn, he lost his job as a chef, so necessity required changes. Friends and co-workers had been telling him for a long time to make his sauces and sell them at local markets. This was the perfect time to give it a try.

He began operating out of his house but expanded into a commercial kitchen within a year by selling to retailers. With each change in his business, Bautista had to learn something new. Using a commercial kitchen was much different than his own personal kitchen. Putting his product online required learning how to pack and ship products. Each growth spurt required hiring more and more employees and tweaking his recipes to make them more cost-effective. Each step also required learning something new in order for the business to grow.

The purpose of this chapter is to help you understand the basic information you must know as you expand into AI. To begin with, you need an AI system that has the fundamental AI capabilities we discussed previously. These capabilities can then be integrated into each of your business functions to make everything more efficient. But how do you start?

If your goal is to make your business more efficient, then the place to begin is to look at your inefficiencies. Don't' start with what you do well; start with what doesn't work. Make an honest assessment. Determine which business function is the most inefficient today. Is it your recruiting and hiring? Or the finance team? Perhaps it's the marketing folks. The area you identify as the weakest should be the starting point for your AI system.

My area of weakness when I decided to write a book on AI was obvious. I know all about the subject, that wasn't a problem. What I didn't know was the process of writing a book. That's where I started.

Your AI Goal

Now that you have identified the area where you want to begin implementing AI, the first step is to create clear, measurable goals to help you stay the course. These goals are statements of what you want AI to deliver for your business. A clear, measurable goal is not an aspirational statement like:

- Improve our speed of hiring
- Reduce the cash collection cycle
- Increase conversion ratio on our E-commerce website
- Reduce manual labor costs

Since these statements are not associated with a numerical statistic, it's not possible to track and measure success. How do you know if you are accomplishing these things? So,

- Instead of saying – Improve our speed of hiring, it should say – Improve monthly hires from 10 to 15 engineers.
- Instead of saying – Reduce the cash collection cycle, it should say – Bring down the cash collection cycle from 83 days to 60 days.
- Instead of saying – Increase conversion ratio on our E-commerce website, it should say – Increase conversion ratio from 1.5% to 3%.
- Instead of saying -- Reduce manual labor costs, it should say – Cut down manual data entry team from 128 to 100.

Once you have a clearly defined goal for your AI system, you are ready to begin implementing it into your business.

Why Do You Need This Goal?

Like everything else about your business, you can't simply decide you want to do something, and then it happens. An AI system must be trained and configured for specific outcomes. In order to do its work, an AI system needs three basic things.

Signals

The term "signals" describes measurements or dimensions that help a system understand what is occurring. In relation to the above-mentioned goal of improving hiring, the following explains the necessary signals.

Information about past resumes where
- You scanned and found not relevant
- You scanned, but the candidates could not clear the interview
- Candidates cleared interviews and were offered a job
- Candidates received the offer but did not join
- Candidates received the offer, joined, but did not do well
- Candidates joined and performed amazingly well.

Details about interviewers
- Who has interviewed rock star candidates in the past
- Pass and Rejection rates

Sources where candidates came from

- *LinkedIn*
- Recruiters
- Employee Referrals
- Campus Hires

These details concerning resumes, interviews, and sources, serve as signals for your AI system.

Data

The term "data" describes how these signals interact with each other. This could be things like past invoice and payment history for a specific customer. It might also be a collection of resumes for a job opening, or result assessment sheets detailing how the candidates performed during each of the discussion rounds and if they accepted the offer or not.

To put it in human terminology, signals are the senses and data is the experience. For example, the first time you encounter something might be with the sense of touch, but experience will identify it as either hot or cold. The signals tell the AI system what matters, and the data tells how the signals relate to one another.

Once you have a clear, measurable goal, you can then decide which signals and data will inform your AI system learning process. Once it analyzes the past data, it will form a hypothesis of what works and what doesn't work. This hypothesis is then tested to see if it can move the needle. After several iterations of rinse and repeat, the system will begin to narrow down what works.

At that point, the system is ready to provide some initial results about what it thinks will work to help achieve your goal. You can take the suggestions to the accounts department or your HR team to see how it works.

Feedback

The final, and perhaps most crucial piece of information is to let the AI system know if its recommendations worked or not. Without feedback, the system will not evolve. Although that sounds simple, I have come across many businesses that do not know the value of this feedback. They take the output from the AI engine but never think about informing the system of success or failure.

Consequently, the system assumes everything is fine, and there is no need to improve or evolve. Every segment of your business is enhanced with feedback. It's crucial to know what works and what doesn't work, what customers think, and what has contributed to successes and failures. The same is true with your AI system. The more feedback you offer, the closer the final result will be to what you desire.

What If You Do Not Have a Clear Goal?

I have come across situations where the business was convinced they need to begin using AI, but they don't know where to start. Everything seemed to be working fine, nothing other than business as usual and certainly nothing causing anyone to lose sleep. Since they don't want to miss the AI bus, they want to try it somewhere. Where do they start?

In such cases, there are two possible approaches:

Start with the Data

The best recommendation would be to start where you have the greatest amount of data. It might be in the form of emails, documents, videos, customer conversation, user behavior, or just numbers. That data can also live outside the digital world, for example, reams of old legal documents stacked in the legal team's office. Digitizing this data is much easier today than it was five years ago. Within this data lies hidden intelligence and patterns that may not be obvious to you. Your AI system can start distilling this data and run experiments that can let you see your business from an entirely new perspective. It's like those unexpected moves that Alpha Zero makes like exposing the King in the middle of the chessboard. It makes those moves because it does not go by conventional wisdom. It learns by doing.

Start with Your Spending on People

If you don't want to start with data, you can begin with functions that involve extensive human labor that needs low-level cognitive skills like listening, reading, looking at pictures, etc. Or another possibility is where many human touch points happen like customer support or store managers. If you choose one of these, your AI goal should be efficiency—better, faster, and cheaper. This can provide a good starting point on your journey to becoming an AI-enabled enterprise.

Companies that use AI extensively in their systems today are already far ahead of their competition. From the moment you turn on your computer and go to *Amazon's* website, AI is hard at work. You first discover recommended products based on past purchases and searches. As soon as you focus on a specific item needed, you are directed to several products that are the best fit for your preferences based on what *Amazon* has learned about you.

Once you order the item, further use of AI kicks in to facilitate shipping the product to your house. Robots whiz around the warehouse specifically chosen based on the availability of the product and most advantageous for shipping to your location. All of this is controlled by AI up to the point of the delivery driver photographing the package placed at your front door. All of that data is then available for the next time you turn to *Amazon* for shopping.

If you're just beginning the journey of utilizing AI, this example is far down the road. However, you'll never get there until you start using AI in your own business. As you can see from the book you hold in your hand, I learned how to write a book. It's probably not the best book ever written on AI, but at least I'm further down the road than I was before.

Part II

**Business Functions and AI – A Collection of
Short Business Stories**

Chapter 5:

AI-enabled HR

Riya oversees Human Resources for a billion-dollar technology company with a global workforce consisting of 30,000 employees. It was just a few years ago that her team included 250 HR managers and associates that took care of recruitment, employee grievances, policy compliance, training, and safety. Things have changed. Riya now works with 40 people and her company's new AI engine named Colin.

Colin is the initial point of contact for everyone needing help from the HR team. When new employees are required, or an existing employee is about to leave or requests training, the request is sent to Colin. Colin manages more than ten thousand interactions every day. Eighty percent of those transactions are handled competently. What that means is that when a response is received from Colin, the employees give a "thumbs up" and have no need for further clarification.

Of the remaining interactions, half of them Colin has an idea of how to respond but is unsure. He drafts a best guess next action and puts it in the queue for Riya's team to review and teach him. At that point, a team member can either accept Colin's proposed action or do something completely different. Either way, Colin learns from the feedback and seeks to improve.

Colin has no idea about the final ten percent of interactions. They are either new issues he has never seen before or sensitive. These interactions are neatly organized into queues based on its understanding and given to Riya's team to manage.

The following are some ways that Colin manages the 80% of interactions it has aced.

Recruitment

The company is on an aggressive growth path, and its technology lead automation business has skyrocketed in the last few years. Nearly all of the company's teams are experiencing a high growth phase, always in need of outstanding, new talent. Colin helps find that talent.

The recruitment process usually begins when someone completes a form on the company's HR portal opening a new position. In addition, some people chat with Colin to accomplish this task. Once this is done, Colin quickly checks HR records to determine what kind of people have performed well in that role for the team and that particular manager. These candidates are analyzed according to experience, companies where they worked in the past, and critical skills. From the feedback form submitted previously by the hiring manager, Colin also knows what appeals to this manager. For example, if Colin knows their head of engineering, Kendall, consistently praises people for their curiosity.

Armed with data from the company, Colin scans recruitment portals for candidates seeking jobs. It grabs their profile and quickly evaluates them against the skills known to be important to this job. When appropriate, it reviews the candidates' *LinkedIn* profile and their received recommendations. This might reveal that some of the recommendations reference curiosity as a key trait, which would make the candidate a good fit for the manager.

Colin reviews 100 profiles for engineering roles at a time because it knows this hit rate will work for the engineering jobs and the hiring manager. Colin has developed an experience-based evaluation matrix for each profile that sorts out the best match. Once the first 100 eligible candidates are sorted, Colin identifies the top three for the hiring manager and asks which candidate she would like to meet. When the hiring manager selects a candidate, let's call her Teresa, because the manager likes her experience and relevant skills, Colin begins the outreach plan to get Teresa to join the team.

The first step of the outreach plan is to send an email to Teresa. The email is designed to speak directly to her. Colin maintains a video archive of the company's current employees and selects one that will click with Teresa. The email is sent to explain why it has reached out to her and about the dimensions where she scored in Colin's evaluation. For example, the email will focus more on hard work and learning new technologies when it sees the candidate share or like posts of new technologies. The email also includes a relevant video testimonial of a current employee with a similar background.

If Colin gets no response in two days, it sends out a couple of follow-up emails before moving on to the next candidate.

Once Teresa shows interest, Colin schedules time on the hiring manager's calendar and orders a Lyft to deliver the candidate at the designated time. One of Riya's local teammates is also advised of the appointment and is on standby to hear feedback on the candidate.

Riya's team processes the feedback on the candidate, negotiates the compensation, and asks Colin to send an offer letter. Once Colin receives acceptance of the offer, Teresa will be enrolled for an orientation program. Colin also orders work equipment for the new employee and sends out benefits administration forms.

At the conclusion of her first week on the job, Teresa may be surprised to find an email from Colin. It asks about her satisfaction with her new workplace and if she has any concerns. A similar email is sent to the hiring manager asking about Teresa. Comparable emails will be sent after a month and then after a quarter.

The feedback is valuable to allow Colin to continue to learn and improve identifying and recruiting future candidates.

Talent Development

Mandatory training is required for every new employee in Riya's company. The training covers everything from orientation to security practices, all the necessary things employees are expected to know. Colin tracks each employee's compliance by ensuring they have enrolled in the training and submitted feedback once complete.

It also reaches out to employees periodically to determine if they need further training. Most employees request training on new technologies that strike their curiosity and anything new they need to learn. Colin collates this data and builds a prioritized list of training. For the most requested instruction, Colin seeks to determine if someone within the company wants to conduct the training. Past experience reveals that employees prefer training by internal experts rather than full-time, professional trainers.

Once a trainer is secured, Colin sends out the details of the training and trainer to Sue, the company's training coordinator. Sue assists first-time trainers in understanding the do's and don'ts of the process. If no internal trainers are available, Sue works with professional trainers and schedules the required sessions.

Goals

Along with the remainder of the management team, Riya makes her goals commitment every quarter to the company's board and CEO. Colin and Riya work together to make sure their team delivers on quarterly obligations. Since the company is experiencing exponential growth, the HR team has steep targets for hiring and getting new engineers onboard.

Colin has determined that in order to onboard as many employees as the company needs, each hiring manager must conduct more than 45 candidates every month.

Clearly, there is no practical way to hit this goal. Based on the feedback, Riya decides that to reach her goals, she will need to acquire a few small companies. Instead of interviewing numerous individuals, hiring managers can participate in doing technical due diligence for a small team and onboard a large team quickly.

Since they are only interested in their talent, not in acquiring a company for its technology or revenue, they seek companies that have not grown in the last few years and have small teams. Taking a list of skills that interested them, Colin sets to work to scout out companies that fit these criteria.

The first step is to work through a list of companies on *LinkedIn* to determine teams that are of the ideal size. Then the individual profiles of engineers are reviewed to get a better understanding of the company's culture and pick up the employee's perspective. A short list of companies is compiled for Riya to evaluate.

Riya chooses four companies for further consideration and then involves her corporate development team. She is confident that one of these four companies will help fulfill her quarterly goals.

If Colin had hands, Riya would have high-fived him today.

Some Real Life References

Ten or fifteen years ago, if you went shopping for a new car, the salesman immediately asked what kind of vehicle you wanted. You would describe the model, perhaps color, and desired features. Taking that information, the salesman would select which cars to show. Ramp up that same process exponentially, and you have what most companies do today with information. They collect as much data as possible about us and then try to predict, and in some cases change, our behavior. When you watch a show on *Netflix*, it determines what other shows it should recommend to you. I'm sure they also use this data to decide what kind of shows they should produce as a part of their original content. And even before an idea hits the shooting floor, they should be able to predict how many hits it will get.

HR companies are no different. They have also started using AI and Machine Learning to solve complex HR problems related to hiring, retention, and employee engagement. A lot of HR management companies have begun rolling out personalized learning systems. It uses the same principle of gathering data about a person to put them in optimal situations. Personalized learning is being used by many large companies as a way to keep employees more engaged but putting them in positions that are more interesting to them. This, of course, improves their performance and strengthens their loyalty to the company.

Workday, another HR Software company, has an AI system that they call "Workday People Analytics." This tool promises to give executives a better understanding of their workforce by leveraging AI machine learning that creates metrics that are explained by creating narratives called stories. Advantages include automated pattern-detection that sees things not recognized by the human eye. The machine learning is also able to make predictions about important issues. These stories not only tell executives what is happening but also provide insight into why it's happening.

As long as companies need employees, AI will be a powerful tool to help get the right people in the best positions.

Chapter 6:

AI-enabled Sales

Pete is a consultant for a large Oil and Natural Gas company. They are searching for a company to help analyze thousands of documents with oil refinery layouts to determine which components are being used and at what refineries. By using *Google*, Pete found a company that claims to make sense of a variety of engineering drawings. Pete clicked on the link and found himself at their homepage.

Pete did not find anything notable about the website; it is like most other corporate websites, it's unremarkable. There is a description of what they do and who they have done it for, and a few mentions from clients raving about their work. As Pete browsed the site for relevant information, a chat window popped up. To prepare himself from being badgered by "what do you need?" or "can I help?" messages, he quickly jumped to another page.

He found some information about extracting data from engineering drawings and noticed as the bot prompted with, "What kind of engineering drawings do you have?" This was a much better question than, "What do you need?" Pete had extensive experience watching these bots unravel at anything beyond the most basic instructions, so he decided to amuse himself for a few minutes.

He typed "oil refinery drawings" in the chat window and prepared for a response that said something like, "Sorry, I don't understand what you mean."

Instead, the chatbot said, "Cool, we do a lot of those. What do you want to extract from these drawings? Components information, layout information, or aging information?"

That got Pete's attention. He was prepared for a long monologue with a salesperson about what engineering drawings for oil refineries look like and how they work. He was pleasantly surprised to "talk" to someone who already knew about the subject. He didn't hesitate to type next to the blinking cursor: "Component Information."

"Sure, we can do that," was the reply from the bot. "Do you have a master list of all the components that you would like this information extracted and verified against?"

"Yes, we do," responded Pete as he was getting excited about the opportunity.

"Cool. Let me show how we extract data from these documents," was the next message. The bot flashed a link to a video of the process using documents similar to the ones Pete had. "Take a look at this video and let me know once you are done or if you have any questions."

After a short time, the bot chimed in, "Would you like to try one of your own documents to see how our extraction works?

"Yeah, sure!"

"Cool. You can upload your document here" as the bot shared a webpage link. "But I do have a small disclaimer—this extraction has not seen your data yet, so its accuracy might not be great. We will make it a lot better when you sign up."

The bot waited for Pete to examine the results and respond. Finally, he typed, "This does not seem to be a good job of handwritten text. Do you have a demo of handwritten text?"

"Sorry, no one has asked me that before," came the reply. "Let me grab someone who can answer that for you. Can you please hold for a second?"

After a short while, another agent joined the conversation. "Hi, my name is Joshua. I heard you had a project requiring extracting handwritten text. How can I help?"

Starting From the Start

Pete's interaction was with Xavier, the company's AI engine that focuses on sales. On a typical day, Xavier interacts with a few hundred people through the company's website, qualifies leads and sets up tens of meetings with sales reps, following-up on another hundred conversations, and keeps tab of the company's revenue growth. Working with the company's sales arm, Xavier reports to Sherry, the global head of sales.

Sherry has been with the company for nearly a dozen years since she moved from Georgia. In her late forties, Sherry is what you might expect to find with a woman from the south. She's pleasant, friendly, and hard-working. Her extrovert personality has allowed her to succeed in sales and her time with the company has demonstrated her capabilities as a leader. She loves the travel that comes with the job.

The company has customers in Europe, Australia, and New Zealand, as well as the United States. Sherry had a team consisting of 110 reps with quotas sprinkled around the globe. Most of them reached out to prospective customers via email, *LinkedIn*, and phones to generate leads for the company.

Statistically, out of 100 potential customers contacted, the reps got a response from five to ten. Of these respondents, usually one or two were interested in what the company offered. As you can imagine, this was high pressure, high-intensity chaos.

That has all changed with Xavier on board. Sherry now runs the entire operation with a team of 27. They are successful even though the targets have increased. The efficiencies that Xavier has brought to her world enables her to achieve higher numbers with fewer reps.

Lead Qualification

The initial point of contact for a prospect is Xavier. Its job is to ensure that the right type of prospect receives a red-carpet welcome, and those who are not a good fit are turned away politely. This allows the sales team to spend their time with prospects who are likely to turn into customers. Xavier achieves this by asking relevant questions through emails and chat conversations on the company's website.

More importantly, it follows up on every lead sent to the sales team for feedback if the rep felt the lead was qualified or not. When the rep determines the prospect is not a good fit, she writes a couple of sentences explaining the decision. Every month, Xavier sifts through this feedback to determine if there are new questions that he should ask when speaking to prospects. This feedback allows Xavier to continually improve.

Predictive Scoring and Lead Routing

Xavier was given access to a massive amount of data concerning prospects contacted by the sales team in the past, along with the results of those conversations. From this data, it determined the type of prospect that makes a great customer where the company's solutions shine, which customer segments are more price sensitive, which verticals have the longest sales cycle, and other categories. The system also has access to after-sale data which explains the type of customers that scale and increase their spending with the company.

In addition, Xavier analyzes the situation from the other side of the coin—the sales reps. It has intelligence about which reps have the highest success ratios with different types of prospects, solutions, or regions. This is important for knowing how to channel which prospects to which sales reps.

Xavier continually runs small experiments with this data to determine the optimal way of securing a lead and then acts as the matchmaker with the rep to achieve the highest rate of success.

Follow Up and Scheduling

All communication between sales reps and prospects is available to Xavier because its job is not complete once initial conversations and commercial discussions are finished. Xavier is also responsible for keeping the prospect engaged. Over the few years that it has been in place, Xavier has learned the art of sending follow-up emails. It is much more than bombarding the prospect with spam.

Sending out emails to follow up with a prospect was a hit or miss for the company. It was sometimes effective but mostly a complete waste of time and effort. Xavier has improved the overall follow-up process by learning a few important things through little experiments that it ran. With a combination of who to send what types of emails at what times and what messaging to include, it has created a secret sauce of getting responses. In the past, follow-up consumed a great deal of time from the reps but now that time is free to spend on more meaningful and productive work.

Post Interaction Engagement

Regardless of how good your company is, not all prospects will become a customer. Some are merely a bad fit for further conversations at the time and others might not have the budget needed to become a customer. Xavier maintains a separate list of these prospects and strives to keep them engaged after their sales conversation. When the company wins a new customer, old prospects are informed about the deal. If a new product or service is released, they are advised. They are kept in the loop.

The purpose is to keep the company's name fresh in the mind of prospects as well as improve relationships with existing customers. Beginning with his first interaction with the website, Pete was engaged until he obtained all the information needed to decide if they could meet his company's needs.

Some Real Life References

The fall of Sears taught the retail world many lessons. Perhaps one of the most significant is that there's no such thing as too big to fail. *Walmart* has woken to that fact and admitted that they became complacent. Now they are striving to reimagine what their business can be, and one of the areas of emphasis is the use of AI. They are using AI to analyze sales data to make predictions and avoid shortages on store shelves. In the past when sales dipped in one of the stores because their suppliers delivered goods late, it would take *Walmart* a few days to figure out what happened.

Now, using their in-house AI and Machine Learning based analytics system, Flight Deck, they learn this within minutes. Galagher Jeff, the company's VP of Merchandising Operations and Business Analytics, was speaking at a retail conference earlier this year when he said, "In retail, we're good at looking backwards. We can tell you the sales from yesterday or the last hour, but we're not good at telling what's coming. The Flight Deck tells us what happens, what drove those business results and what you should do about it." They have also begun using product recommendations generated by AI on their website which is something customers have come to expect from retail sites. *Walmart* is also putting a great deal of research into the possibility of providing grocery delivery to customers. This includes experimenting with self-driving delivery cars.

The company plans to make 2,000 tech hires in the near future, and many of them will be employed working with AI. *Walmart* says they have more data than nearly everyone in the world, so they making massive investments into using that data to grow the business.

Retail giant, Macy's is utilizing an AI-powered shopping assistant available to customers through a mobile phone app. Through the app, customers can ask personalized questions and receive immediate answers. If the customer needs to find the men's suit department, the app will provide directions inside the store. It can also provide answers concerning product assortment and availability.

They are only one of many brands finding ways to incorporate AI into their brick and mortar retail stores. Other applications include allowing advertisers of products carried by retailers to interact with the customers and use gathered data to direct customers to products that they will find interesting.

Chapter 7:

AI-enabled Marketing

Armed with a freshly printed degree in marketing, Judy secured a job with a company in Chicago. Although the big city was an adjustment for Judy who grew up in a medium-sized Midwestern city, she now found herself feeling at home. She learned how to maneuver the transit systems around the city over the past six years, and her small apartment was finally decorated in her own personal style.

She was hired to work in the marketing department and given the assignment to develop creative ways to sell a wide selection of products and services. Judy turned out to be a talented marketer. Her salary grew commensurate with the creative sales campaigns she designed. The small company where she was first hired six years ago was now a rapidly growing brand that was becoming known worldwide.

Management rightfully gave appropriate credit to Judy, and now she finds herself as the chief storyteller of the company. She is responsible for engagingly communicating with customers and prospects. Judy has a team of 38 marketers. They are responsible for all the products her company sells online. This includes dresses, shoes, electronics, books, and numerous other items. Think of them as a smaller version of *Amazon*.com.

Judy's work begins when her company sources a product from the manufacturer. Her team is responsible for describing the product, ensuring the photos and specifications along with all the other detailed information is accurate and precise. The products are then published on the company's website and to hundreds of affiliates who are responsible for driving traffic to the website. Once a potential customer lands on the site, the marketing team is responsible for the customer finding the desired product quickly and that the purchase is smooth and easy.

In addition to the affiliates who send traffic to the website, Judy secures a great deal of traffic from paid ads on related sites. Every month her team runs promotions to acquire new customers.

In addition to making products appear appealing on the website, there are two other aspects of Judy's work. One is to get customers who have been to the site previously, to return and make additional purchases. This involves making the website a good experience for customers. The other is to be continually up-selling and cross-selling products. When customers purchase a product, there are often other products that are a natural fit, and it's Judy's job to encourage customers to consider additional items before checking out.

One of the tools to encourage customers to return to their online shop is email campaigns. A benefit of selling online is that it provides access to customer information, specifically email addresses. These email addresses provide the opportunity to keep in touch with customers on a continuing basis. One approach is to use email campaigns. These campaigns can be customized according to previous purchases made by the customer.

Upselling requires understanding the relationship between products. If a customer purchases a pair of shoes, they might also be interested in a matching purse, or if they bought a computer, it's likely they will need a monitor as well. Making all of this happen is a task assigned to Judy's team.

It wasn't that long ago there was massive chaos among Judy's team. There were more than 120 members of the group who had the task of staying on top of the product catalog. There was a continual rush to provide the latest information of everything in the catalog which often led to mistakes and duplications. For example, on one occasion, a team member put a new product in a category titled, "Back to School." At the same time, a similar product was tagged with "Back 2 School."

One of the biggest challenges Judy faces is taking the current information available from customer purchases and translating it into predictions of future trends. Primarily, she is expected to know what customers will want in six months. The reason this is crucial to the success of the company is that purchasers need to stock the items that will sell, so it's imperative they all stay on the same page. In other words, Judy doesn't merely sell whatever they can purchase at a bargain price, she helps determine the products they will buy in the first place.

It's obviously a daunting task, and you can see why 120 team members were needed and why they got in each other's way. That all changed last year when a new member joined Judy's team. Its name is Catherine, and it is the company's new AI engine. Catherine's efficiencies allowed Judy to optimize her team's work and cut the size down from 120 to 38. One of the most useful tasks Catherine performs is the paid Ads. This was Judy's largest spending item in previous years.

If you use *Google* or *Facebook* (or numerous other sites), you have seen and possibly used paid Ads. It describes those small ads that show up on your computer screen and are targeted specifically to you. For example, if you do a *Google* search for dog food, don't be surprised if you see advertisements on your *Facebook* page for the next couple of days promoting various dog food products. These searches trigger Ads that are only charged to the sponsoring company when a user clicks on the Ad. Consequently, they are often referred to as "pay-per-click."

Sellers purchase keywords at an ad auction by bidding how much they will pay for a particular search term. For example, Judy's company sells a large number of cooking utensils. They can benefit from customers searching for slow cookers, cookware, measuring spoons, or other cooking supplies. They want to attract potential customers for all of these items as well as the more generic term "cookware."

Staying on top of everything happening with *Google* AdWords is a full-time job requiring several employees. Creating and updating Ads based on the value they bring to the website was a constant struggle. On a typical day, they spend thousands of dollars on Ads. Despite the considerable workforce assigned to the task, they often got it wrong. Sometimes they would bid $3 for an Ad click which only had a profit margin of $2. Simply put, they were spending more on customer acquisition than the customer was worth.

Catherine manages all of it with little help. Following the trends, Catherine not only knows what is being searched but can also calculate a winning bid for those words and save money for the company. It ingests the sales data and Ad configurations for analysis. Based on a mix of more than 20 signals, it started optimizing the money spent on Ads to the point that no loss-generating traffic was being acquired. The 25 people previously needed for the task was trimmed to six.

In addition to improving the purchase of terms for Ad Words, Catherine was also given the task of enhancing promotions and campaigns. Similar to Ads, there is a great deal of science behind understanding which customers are most likely to react positively to specific campaigns. A marketing campaign is an organized, strategic effort to raise awareness of the company or promote a product. A campaign can include a variety of media, including emails, print, TV and radio, pay-per-click, and social media.

The success of a campaign depends on the ability to target the right audience with the right message. This requires a thorough analysis of data, and that's why Catherine is so effective. Taking existing knowledge of the product catalog and sales data, it makes hypotheses about what will produce the most success. At the beginning of the experiment, 50 versions of campaigns were tested under the guise of "who likes what." Learning from the experience, Catherine calculated a formula for running automated campaigns. A team of marketers consisting of four people is still needed to design the campaign banners, but that is far fewer than the original thirteen.

Whenever a potential customer searches for an item, they are essentially requesting information that will motivate them to turn into a paying customer. When a well-designed email shows up in their inbox within a few hours or even a couple of days, it's most likely to make a profitable connection. When they are connected to an item that fits their specific tastes and desires, the odds of purchase increase significantly.

To make this happen frequently, Catherine is able to sort through the data and find customers who are the best fit for a campaign. It knows how to sort the information to target customers with specific products meeting their interests. This kind of targeting typically requires hundreds of hours of manpower, but with Catherine, it's done in seconds. The fact that Catherine is continually learning new information, the success rate continually improves.

According to one company's survey, when products are customized the result was a 109% increase in click-throughs to the product page and a 17% increase in additional page visits.

At one time, AI was based on algorithms developed by human programmers providing step-by-step instructions for the computer. However, with machine learning, computers have greater freedom to utilize their capability. Judy discovered that when a customer visited their website, Catherine was able to quickly analyze data and offer products that most appeal to that particular customer.

Catherine is also involved in creating the content for the website. It can take the data about a product and develop descriptions that will appeal to the company's customers. They still employ writers to take Catherine's created content and edit it to make it more free-flowing, but it's much more efficient than a writer starting from scratch.

Each website visit and every purchase provides additional data that Catherine accesses to increase the efficiency of Judy's team. They have gone from spending hours designing and sending out a general email hoping to generate a small percentage of opens and clicks to sending out targeted information to potential customers who are seeking precisely what is being advertised. It's no wonder Judy is considered the chief storyteller for the company.

Some Real Life References

Marketing has a lot more data than other business functions. Almost everything they produce is data—a video ad, brochure, flyer, emails, etc. This data, and how customers behaved with it, can provide massive insights for refining and targeting your message. Coca Cola is pushing their marketing efforts to an entirely new frontier. Coca Cola has indicated that their ads might be made by AI in the near future. They have hired their first Chief Digital Marketing Officer with the plan to discover how AI could replace humans in ad creation. Theoretically, the technology can also handle creating music, writing scripts, social media postings, and media purchases. The company is currently running ads that are personally designed for each recipient that AI selects from a stored media library.

Social media provides an overabundance of marketing insights. There is a surplus of companies that use machine learning and AI for making sense of wisdom of the crowd. Cronycle.com is one such company. Its algorithms boil the ocean of *Twitter* conversations into categories and influencers to identify what is the most relevant conversation around a topic. From biomimicry to politics, they cover everything under the sun and produce amazing insights for marketers to pull out curated content for their messaging, conversations, and distribution.

Many companies are already using AI effectively for marketing. And some ambitious ones like Coca Cola have even grander plans.

Chapter 8:

AI-enabled Legal Services

Aidan is the General Counsel at one of the five largest companies in America. His team of 103 associates is responsible for handling all the legal matters, which for a large company are considerable. These range from relatively simple issues like non-disclosure agreements to complex business transactions necessary for joint ventures, acquisitions, divestitures, and other processes. Also, being a publicly listed company, Aidan is responsible for compliance with SEC regulations and necessary filings.

Although they try to avoid it as often as possible, there are times when Aidan and his team are involved in complex business litigation. This includes the need to sue another business as well as defend their own actions in filings against them.

Aidan introduced a new team member recently—the company's new AI engine known as Jules. Aidan knows better than most that legal documents are complex. More than once he has spoken at a corporate event and said, "If you think technology can replace lawyers then clearly, you do not have the faintest idea about what lawyers do." Aidan was skeptical when Jules was brought in to help his team.

During their last annual strategic planning meeting, it was mandated that all business functions within the company utilize one AI implementation for the year, so Aidan had no choice but to try. He selected the simple work of document assembly as the place to begin. It was the least risky area of his work.

In a typical month, hundreds of people requested Aidan's team provide non-disclosure agreements with external entities. Although they already had a boilerplate version of an NDA, it almost always required alterations. Although this was a simple task, the workload was high volume and kept the legal team busy.

Aidan determined that Jules could chat with the employees requesting the NDA and make the template before sending it out for approval. The changes were simple and based on the purpose of the NDA, type of entity, the identity of the other party, and additional essential information. Although it was a simple task, it significantly reduced the workload on the entire team.

With that initial success, Jules was given the additional responsibility of preparing paperwork for filings. This not only included simple motions for summary judgments but also putting together other documents to be reviewed and changed by members of the legal team. With each change, Jules learned something new about how to write the documents more accurately. Over time, it's accuracy became commendable, and the legal team was freed from a large amount of paperwork.

Jules puts its best foot forward during the discovery process. This has always been the most costly and time-consuming of the legal process and provides a significant place to save money. Lawyers are expected to wade through an enormous pile of physical documentation to determine critical elements of a case. In fact, Aidan's team was already using an e-Discovery tool prior to Jules, but it was limited in capability.

Jules did much more. It began to identify where to look and what questions to ask during discovery. Based on the company's extensive legal history, Jules learned much about what works and what doesn't work for specific types of cases. It also prioritized discovery material for the legal team allowing them to examine the more relevant stuff quicker.

Although Aidan was marginally impressed with Jules' work on NDAs and automated filings, seeing what it could do with discovery turned him into an AI believer. The next step was to turn Jules loose to work on legal research.

Aidan's company used legal information that was made available via the Internet by LexisNexis. They continuously published, updated, and annotated cases. Aidan wanted Jules to solve two problems that he needed to be handled to be successful—time and confidence in the results. His team used to spend countless hours in researching cases and manually going through tons of legal documentation. In fact, Aidan's largest business spend was on legal research work. Jules started processing this data in a fraction of time needed previously. When it found relevant case data, it would show it to a research assistant and get feedback on whether it was relevant or not. This feedback enabled it to become more accurate over time.

The second problem of needing confidence in the results is exacerbated by the preponderance of information available. Aidan was not sure if a researcher knows that everything sought has been found? There was also the unknown of how an individual court or judge will respond to specific information. Jules solved this problem by incrementally building data about different types of cases, judges, and claims. After a while, it gave confidence to Aidan that if LexisNexis had information about anything, Aidan would know how to find it. Jules eliminated a lot of the guesswork in the process.

Aidan has not only been able to reduce the size of his team substantially, but the current team is able to produce better results. The company is saving money with each document produced and court case entered. With the ability to continue learning, Jules' impact will become more and more significant in the future.

Some Real Life References

They say that Lady Justice is blind. You've seen the statue of her holding the scales of justice while wearing a blindfold. While it's true that justice is impartial, it's not always affordable. Many people need simple legal representation but can't afford the cost of a lawyer. Perhaps they need help in traffic court with a couple of parking tickets, or maybe they have a good case to file a lawsuit, but it costs money.

Until AI.

Joshua Browder came up with a way to dispute an abundance of parking tickets. Using AI, he developed a means of challenging the tickets without having to physically do it himself or hire an attorney. The concept has evolved over time to the point of providing a mechanism to file lawsuits.

The process begins when you answer a few questions posed by the chatbot. They are fundamental questions about who you want to sue and the situation. The information is used to compile the documents necessary to file with the courthouse as the plaintiff. The materials include a demand letter and court filing documents. If at some point your presence is required in court, the AI will even generate a script for you to read.

The idea to do this has been floating around for some time, and it's been suggested that AI legal help is impossible. Browder himself admits that he was shocked when people reported winning cases against *Equifax* for mishandling their personal data and awarded judgments of more than $10,000. He also states that half of the people who utilize the system have been successful. It's all provided at no cost to the user.

Not only does the current system exclude the poor who cannot afford a lawyer, but many times, the only beneficiaries of the system are a handful of lawyers. AI can make access to the law available to the average person.

The application has been most used to fight for money like damages from accidents or securing the return of a security deposit. Another category consists of those opposing a corporation over defective products and the consequences of a data breach. It is also being utilized to fight bureaucracy. In the first two years, the AI systems helped appeal more than 160,000 parking tickets handed out in London and New York City.

One of the most substantial expenses in the legal world happens before even going to court. It's the process known as discovery. Much time and effort are expended working through heaps and heaps of documents, emails, contracts, and other paperwork to sort out what's needed for a trial.

The purpose of the discovery process is to allow both sides to share information before trial. This enables the actual trial to proceed smoothly without unnecessary delays. Part of the discovery process is for the plaintiff to obtain information from the other party. Once information about the lawsuit is submitted to the AI system, all the steps to request, locate, and collate the material is handled without human involvement.

Every court case involves a discovery process to some extent. Law firms utilize a complete staff to handle the paperwork and preparations to go to trial. Some estimates place the cost of discovery at nearly $20 billion just in civil cases. AI is a very cost-effective way of reducing these costs and as it's proving to be able to eliminate all costs of simple cases.

The legal system has been hesitant to use AI under the assumption that lawyers couldn't be replaced by machines. However, to expect a computer to eliminate the need for individual lawyers is not the correct approach. The benefit will come once the realization hits that one lawyer utilizing an AI system can do the same work that currently requires multiple lawyers. With the current amount of time and expense used in just the discovery phase of a case, it's obvious that is one area that AI can make a significant improvement.

Chapter 9:

AI-enabled Accounting and Finances

Larry is a typical looking ex-college jock. There's no doubt he was once a well-conditioned athlete, but as he gets closer and closer to age 50, he's added more fat than muscle. Keeping trim has not been easy because, for the past 25 years, Larry's work in accounting has involved many hours sitting behind a desk. However, he's stayed with the same company since graduating from college and has enjoyed a steady rise toward the top of the organizational chart. He is now head of accounting at a Midwest accounting company that helps its customers save money by determining where they have overpaid or not received an appropriate discount or credit.

For many years, Larry's audit work involved reviewing contracts that his customers signed with suppliers and then recording if there was a difference in what was actually paid. It was tedious, going through each contract and checking it against line items in the accounting system. Larry made his money by collecting a percentage of the amount he recovered for his customers. If his work didn't find any unpaid money, then he didn't get paid. Consequently, Larry and his team were under constant pressure to produce.

This changed a few years back. While working with a customer in 2016, he bumped into Albert, one of the purchase managers at the company. Larry and Al met over a casual encounter at the coffee machine. They hit it off because both played football in college. Larry was a large lineman, and Al was a short quick running back who was quite a bit younger and still in good enough shape to play football in a men's league. Their similar backgrounds opened the door for them to talk about several different subjects.

One day, Al happened to mention that the previous year he had negotiated a complicated deal with a supplier. He described spending several days negotiating over emails before eventually arriving at a price favorable to both parties. As he listened, an idea flashed through Larry's mind. He asked to see the correspondence between Al and the supplier, and Al was glad to oblige.

That evening, after his work was complete with his planned analysis and reconciliation with the accounting system, Larry decided to read through the emails. Many of them described sticking points in pricing and others were nothing more than arranging times for phone calls for further discussion. There was even a few explaining how the supplier was waiting for a technical resource person who was in Europe on a three-week vacation.

"Europeans and their vacations," mused Larry to himself.

It took some time, but Larry sifted through 189 emails that night. He found about ten that indicated at least some agreement on discounts. One email concluded that when the buyer spends in excess of $100 million in a year, they receive a five percent discount on all further orders. This one caught his attention, so he printed it out and tucked it inside his organizer. The other nine emails had similar promises of rebates and discounts upon reaching a specific financial milestone. Larry printed them all and kept them together. The plan was to validate the discounts against the actual contracts the next morning.

Larry was excited about the possibility, and that excitement prevented him from a good night's sleep. He dreamed of hitting the jackpot if he discovered that none of the discounts were in the final contract. That would mean a hefty payment for Larry, but he was also anxious because it suggested there might be a bigger problem. Was this simply Albert's problem or was it widespread across the board.

The first thing Larry did the next morning was to validate the 10 emails against the contract. After checking the first three without finding a discrepancy, he began to feel his hopes for a big payday deflate. By the time he reviewed the fourth email his pace had slowed along with his anticipation. However, he didn't give up and continued. A glimmer of hope returned when he found an inconsistency with the fifth and sixth. By the time he completed all ten emails, a total of three discrepancies were evident. Three out of ten doesn't sound like much, but when they added up to nearly two million dollars for his customer which translated to a couple hundred thousand for Larry, he was ecstatic.

At the end of the day, not only did Larry have more money, but he was also convinced there was a more significant problem than this one case. After all, using emails to make these deals is standard practice which suggests mistakes are inevitable. He wanted to follow this same procedure with all of his clients, but that would require wading through millions of emails. Not only would he need a larger team but also greater bandwidth. Calculating the need for 28 additional accountants was a significant investment for Larry.

He began the search for a cheaper alternative to solving this new problem. After spending some time shuffling around on *Google*, Larry discovered a company that processes emails using AI technologies, including Natural Language Processing. Working with this company, they were able to develop a first version assistant for Larry that he fondly named Al, after his new friend Albert. Al began the process of sorting through millions of emails to discover more than 1,000 that his team could verify for missed discounts. On his first assignment, Al did the work of more than 20 accountants and even allowing Larry and his company to do much more work. Larry and Al have not looked back since making their first small fortune auditing emails.

AI has brought significant change to the way accounting teams operate. Historically, their work consisted of creating and processing invoices, purchase orders, and delivery orders. This data was then manually entered into a computer system where it could be coded and transmitted for approval and payment. AI has eliminated the manual processes and automated the workflow. This technology makes it possible for small and medium-sized companies to do things that were possible only with large firms previously.

Larry's team is now using AI to model and extract information from existing documents. This requires AI because the system needs to learn from the data rather than merely relying on rules-based procedural programming. The system can not only discover patterns in the data, but it can also correlate that information to enable predictive analysis.

An additional benefit is that the AI system can identify and interact with suppliers and eliminate the need for team members to perform tasks like intake, coding, and routing. This frees up the accounting team to do analysis, strategy, creative thinking, and decision-making—much more profitable tasks.

Some Real Life References

If you've ever received a detailed bill from a hospital stay, you're aware it can be a complex document. Imagine if you were responsible for keeping track of all the medicines, treatments, and services that were provided. Derek Bang understands this multifaceted situation more than most. He's the chief strategy and innovation officer at Crowe Horwath, one of the largest accounting firms in the country.

He and his team of 20 data scientists have harnessed technology to handle the unique billing problems in the healthcare industry. They created a means of using machine-based learning to sift through the enormous billing systems of health care clients. It flags accounts that have complex and time-consuming processing and reimbursement systems. The technology developed by Crowe Horwath is proactive in dealing with these rather than waiting for the problems to make themselves known. This development saves clients hundreds of man-hours.

Another large accounting firm, Deloitte, is excited about auditors using AI-based applications to quickly conduct assessments of vast real estate holdings or analyze thousands of contracts. This allows for faster, more accurate assessment of the risks faced by large companies.

Bookkeeping can be slow and tedious work. As with any business, time equals money which drives up the cost of services. As a company grows larger, the cost of accounting increases as well. A solution to this problem is software automation. This can mean less time required, less stress, and lower costs, things that are beneficial to any company.

Automated transaction retrieval uses encrypted logins to collect transaction information for your bank account. Through a process of sync and match, transactional amounts are compared to your account which automates bank reconciliation. The software even takes into account transactions that have not yet cleared the bank through a form of AI that generates account data by learning from previous transactions.

It can also create invoices from sales orders and when payment is received, it is matched with the invoice. It also keeps track of unpaid invoices. Simultaneously, the number of items listed on the invoice makes it possible to know when the inventory is running low. Also, it tracks sales opportunities by providing reminders and recording calls and tasks. It is estimated that as much as 90% of regular accounting work can be handled automatically.

In the past, the work of accounting has been one of the most labor-intensive functions of a business. The advent of computers made everything much easier, but it still required a human physically capturing the data and entering it into the computer. However, AI has taken it to an entirely new level. Not only can automation capture the data, but AI can also provide analysis of data to the extent that is unavailable without machine learning.

Chapter 10:

AI-enabled Logistics and Operations

Operating a mid-sized electrical component manufacturing company would not have been Drew's choice of
occupation when he was young. But life doesn't always
turn out like we expect. His father started the company
and Drew worked there as soon as he was old enough to
be of value in the shop. His father taught the importance
of being responsible which was a bonus to the education
he received about manufacturing.

Drew continued working at the shop through high
school and even while attending a local college. By the
time he graduated, it was only a natural progression that
he took over the business when his father died unexpect-
edly. The company was doing well, and Drew was actually enjoying his work.

His customers are primarily construction companies
that use enormous amounts of electrical components for
large projects like sports stadiums and apartment com-
plexes. The construction company puts architects and de-
signers to work studying the plans and layout for a project
to determine how many and what type of electrical components are needed for the entire project. This information is shared with several parties including general contractors, inspectors, and suppliers like Drew's company.

The document that concerns Drew's company explains the design and electrical specifications of all electrical layouts in the structure. It's typically several hundred pages in length. Upon receiving the document, Drew's team studies the numbers to calculate the components needed. Once that decision is made, the next step is to determine which ones they manufacture, and which will need to be sourced from other partners. This process typically requires two to four weeks. At that point, they provide a quote for the new project.

Numerating, locating, and pricing the number of electrical components needed for an apartment complex or sports stadium is a massive undertaking. Not only is it time-consuming, but the cost in man-hours is enormous. The cost of this process has to be written into the bid submitted for the job.

For several years, Drew's company has been stable, maintaining a slow rate of growth each year. However, earlier this year, he decided it was time to move the needle for growth and increase company revenue. He was ready to move things forward. Drew is a good manager of his people, so he knew better than to impose this opportunity on his staff. He scheduled a meeting with his leadership team to discuss ideas. They were all on board with the idea of growth, but they also knew the problems it would bring.

After several hours of discussion, it was apparent the bottleneck that kept it from happening was processing the documents. If they were going to go after more projects and jobs, they would have to find a faster way to handle more orders. Drew and his team decided the first step was to visit with a couple of their better customers and find a way to make the paperwork more efficient.

Upon returning to his office after the meeting, Drew had a message to call Alan, one of their biggest customers. Perfect timing, he thought, so he placed the call. After dealing with the customer's question, Drew explained the project initiated by his team to expedite the paperwork process. Alan was even more excited than Drew and quickly volunteered to help in any way possible.

The next day he had lunch scheduled with Maggie who was the CEO of Acme Electrical, another one of Drew's customers. At the restaurant, they also discussed the need for streamlining the process. Maggie shared how their company was looking into doing some things with Artificial Intelligence, but she didn't understand enough about it to even be an encouragement to her own company.

During an email exchange with another of his customers that afternoon, Drew found another willing partner. All three expressed a desire to find a way to better use their systems to communicate with Drew's company. The hope was that it would not only be profitable for Drew but for everyone involved.

Armed with his new analysis, Drew set about the task of locating a technology partner to help automate the process of extracting information from RFP documents. Every company he approached assured him that what he wanted was not a big deal and they could do it in a matter of a few days. However, when he handed them a few sample documents to review, they all came back with an excuse.

One of them explained, "This has very complex tables, beyond what we do."

Another contributed, "There is no consistency in these documents, even the ones from the same builder. You need some patterns in order to automate this."

Drew had learned from his father not to get discouraged when you have a good idea, so he kept looking. One afternoon he was visiting with a college roommate who works in retail. As Drew explained what he needed for his company, his friend Andy realized it was similar to a situation facing his company last year. They were struggling with delays in securing merchandise to fill orders when wholesalers suddenly told them they were out of stock. They discovered an AI company that solved their problem. He shared the company information with Drew when they departed.

Drew contacted them early the next morning, and in a short time, he was listening as they explained that until a few years ago, it was not possible to automatically understand documents that did not have any consistent forms or patterns. However, they had made advances with AI which positioned them uniquely to solves problems like this. He offered an example of how they automatically extract information from the layout of documents for oil refineries. These documents were much more complicated than the ones utilized by Drew's company.

Drew's team worked with this company and put together an AI engine that processed the documents. They were all amazed when it handled the first one in less than a minute. They were equally impressed by the accuracy.

Because of this speed and accuracy, they named their new AI engine, "Flash," in honor of the superhero.

They continually pushed Flash's limits with additional experiments and began using it for optimization across the board. After mastering automation, Flash's next job was to predict demand to optimize production and reduce the cycle for order delivery.

In early August of last year, everything came to a near shutdown at Drew's factory. Everyone strives to be careful on the manufacturing floor, but it often takes some time for new employees to grasp the importance of following procedures. A young man named Mark, who had been with the company for five weeks, wasn't paying close attention and drove a forklift over boards from a packing crate lying on the floor. The forklift tipped over, and Mark's leg was trapped underneath. When they were able to get the vehicle off Mark, it was apparent his leg was seriously injured. It was determined that a major tendon had been cut in half and it was unlikely he would regain full use of his leg.

Drew's entire team rallied around the young man, visiting him in the hospital, providing help and encouragement to his family. The expenses were covered by insurance but Drew felt like they needed to do more to prevent another accident in the future. As they considered ways to make the plant safer, one of the first suggestions was to utilize their new friend Flash.

It was suggested that workers be equipped with smart glasses to capture information about problems or potential accident sites. As the employees wore the glasses on the manufacturing floor, Flash analyzed real-time images and videos from the lenses and warned employees of dangers and problem areas. Also, it was able to identify unattended equipment or raw material lying on the floor that created a potentially harmful situation. Not only did Flash help prevent accidents, but it was also a constant reminder to employees to be more aware of their surroundings. The bottom line is that the manufacturing building was a safer place.

Roger, one of the company managers, suggested another experiment for Flash. He noticed they were receiving numerous returns from the field for one particular component. It had only been released a few months earlier, but the return rate was higher than it should have been. It looked similar to an older version of the part and contractors were messing up the installation instructions, confusing the two components.

From the lessons learned about the smart glasses, Roger suggested offering their smart glasses to their larger contractors and then guiding them in how to handle the component. The installer could hold it in front of the glasses, Flash would identify it correctly, and then convey the proper installation instructions. Drew took the idea one step further and added a post-installation checklist. Once installation was complete, the glasses would prompt the installer with a short checklist to verify that all the safety steps have been followed.

Once the concept was developed, they made it available to one of their largest customers in hopes it would benefit both companies. The contractor was impressed with the work of his installers. It saved time because they didn't have to replace the incorrectly installed part and return it for a refund. In the construction business, as in most businesses, time is money. Flash was not only making money for Drew's company, but it was also making an impact with their customers as well.

Each success generated suggestions for further uses of this new technology. An idea that became a favorite with the construction companies was extending vision capabilities beyond employees. They wired a drone to connect with Flash to analyze live videos of construction sites. At the conclusion of each work day, the drone hovered over the construction site and completed a safety inspection. Once again, the result was a safer workplace and money was saved.

Flash proved to be a highly profitable decision for Drew's company. What began as a simple desire by Drew to grow the company was exceeding his highest hopes. For the past three years, the company has surpassed its own growth records, and with the continued help of their AI system, expectations for the future are even higher.

Some Examples From Real Life

One of the most well-known examples of AI in the area of logistics and operations can be found at an *Amazon* warehouse. They use robots and conveyors to move products around from storage to shipment. When an order is placed, it's routed to a warehouse. A robot goes to the bin where the item is stored, loads it up, and puts it on the conveyor. From there it is carried through the process where it is packaged, and postage attached. This is one of the keys that has allowed *Amazon* to grow so enormous.

AI's unique use of robots can also be found in numerous *Walmart* stores. They are using robotic floor scrubbers. The company has 704 million square feet of floor space that needs to be mopped, and the robots are expected to free up workers to do other jobs around the store. The robots depend on sensors to scan for obstructions and shoppers. Robots are also being utilized to unload delivery trucks, check items on the shelves, check price labels on products, and even select items to fill online grocery orders.

A similar change is occurring at Giant Food Stores where the robot's primary purpose is to roam the store and point out hazards for store staff to clean up. The robot, named Marty, has been built to resemble a human with a face and a speaking feature. The plan is to expand the usage to include shelf-scanning for out-of-stock items. They actually encourage customers to interact with the robot.

Part III

Business Strategy & AI

Chapter 11:

The Human Aspect–People and Relationships

In 2014, although it took a circuitous route, I managed to secure a meeting with the CEO of a large department store chain in the United States. I have fond memories of that meeting for many reasons. Foremost, it's not easy for a startup to secure a meeting with the CEO of such a large company in person and the path to making it happen was quite memorable. I located one of my existing customers who has happy with our technology and convinced him to log on to his Harvard alumni network and source me a couple of meetings with large retailers. Also, he connected me with a few venture capital companies. Although most of the retail meetings went nowhere, one of the investors I met with arranged the meeting with this CEO.

A second memorable aspect of the meeting was that after this CEO agreed to a meeting, he connected me with his executive assistant. She provided a date that was four months out since that was the first free time he had on his calendar. I have never had to wait that long for a meeting, but I was still eager for it to happen. When I arrived, I was ushered into a private conference room attached to his office. It was his own private conference room that he used for meetings, and it was impressive. The whole building was massive and memorable. His office overlooked the San Francisco Bay providing an unforgettable view. I had worked with company CEOs in the past, but I had never seen an office set up quite as impressive.

After introductions, I quickly got to the point and showed him and his team what our AI engine was able to do. His initial response was, "You know, most startups that pitch to us tell us that we need to do something new. The beauty of your platform is that you use existing data that we already have instead of requiring us to do something new. I love it. Let's do it!"

He made sure I was introduced to the EVP of Marketing who connected me with one of his managers since that was the team that would use our product directly. However, this is where things began to go awry. This person ran a team of about 200 people whose job was to manually curate data. Besides taking a long time and spending a big budget, they also made frequent errors because of the tedious nature of the work. I showed her how our engine would dramatically cut down the manual labor, reduce turnaround time, and improve accuracy and left feeling like I had hit a home run. We had produced convincing data showing the company is losing a few million dollars every year because of inaccuracies. In addition, there was the cost of 200 employees doing the work. Our solution would solve both of these problems.

She led me to believe that she was impressed and was eager to integrate our solution into their system. She then went on to explain that her current schedule was completely packed, and we would need to wait until the next quarter to start. I understood, and it was not a problem.

When the next quarter started, she did the same thing. The quarter after that, she said she had an organization-wide system freeze and no changes were allowed. For two years she stalled our implementation, and it became clear that her goal was to protect the jobs of her team members. Finally, I tried to go up the chain to get new directives, but she steadily went out of her way to find a reason why it could not be done at this time.

Even today, I'm amazed at that office and at the fact that we could not get them to use our engine even after having the nod of approval from the CEO and EVP. As comedian Chris Rock once said, "I am not saying it's right—but I understand."

I understand the natural, human tendency—the goodness in humans—that makes us watch out for the people we care about—friends, family, colleagues, and fellow citizens. This value is what makes us what we are.

But the question is what does this have to do within a book about AI-enabled automation?

Everything!

Throughout the book, I've shared stories about key executives in companies who have used automation. You have read how they used AI to make departments more efficient and profitable. You might have noted that one of the impacts of automation is a reduction in jobs. Teams that relied on manpower in the past have been reduced with AI doing much of the work. In the future, numerous jobs that require low level human cognitive skills will be automated using AI. That doesn't necessarily mean unemployment. But it does mean doing new things and learning new skills.

Recently, I was fascinated by a television program that cited research data about ATMs and bank teller jobs. When you think about ATMs and Bank Teller jobs, your first logical conclusion might be that ATMs eliminated the need for bank tellers leaving many bank employees unemployed. However, that is not the case. Back in 1985, the United States reported 60,000 ATMs and 485,000 bank tellers. The number of machines increased significantly to 352,000 by 2002, but the number of bank tellers also increased to 527,000. The Bureau of Labor Statistics predicts the number of tellers will continue to grow in the future.

The omnipresent ATMs are doing the mundane activities related to depositing and withdrawing money which frees up bank tellers to do things that are more profitable to the banks. They have much more time to spend up-selling and cross-selling services to their customers.

Retail banks began adopting computers in their offices when I was 12 or 13 years old. I clearly remember the panic felt by one of my uncles who worked at a bank. To him, the computer was the beginning of the end. He would bemoan, "There will no longer be a need for people like me. The computers are coming, and they're going to take over everything!" That same uncle would eventually retire from the same bank where he has worked for more than 35 years.

Do You Really Have a Choice?

In my younger years, I made countless trips to Borders, Circuit City, and Blockbuster. These stores are out of existence today, although I read the other day there is still one Blockbuster store in business in Bend, Oregon.

During the early dot com era, the wave of disruption that burst through the business world changed everything about their business and made their business model un-viable. All of them were replaced by companies that did not have to bear the baggage of old thinking, systems, or business acumen.

If you operate a company that depends on human labor for low skill-level tasks, choosing to avoid automation means a new rival will come along and put you out of business. Starting fresh, a new company doesn't have the same constraints that hinder your mature business. The low cost of automation and economies of scale means they can provide the same product or service much cheaper to your customers. You know what that means. In a short time, you will be out of business.

That's exactly what *Amazon* and *Netflix* did to Borders, Circuit City, and Blockbuster. Their new business model was not slowed by the constraints of the old world—physical stores and in-store labor. Consequently, they have disrupted long-running businesses out of existence. If you decide not to get on the automation train, one of your competitors or a new start-up certainly will.

Let me tell you the story of *Metromile*.

At my son's birthday party a few years back, one of the Dads I met introduced me to *Metromile*. He explained that it was a unique way of providing car insurance. Rather than a flat monthly charge, the cost is calculated by the number of miles you drive. The company targets those who drive fewer than 1,000 miles a month. To keep track of the mileage, a device is installed in the vehicle. The months that you drive less means that you pay less.

The company was founded in 2011 and now operates in about a half dozen states. Not only does the device installed in your vehicle keep track of mileage, but it can also determine what happens in the event of an accident. When the car owner submits a claim after the accident, within seconds, the system is able to confirm the description of the crash and approve payment for damages within seconds. When the AI system, named Ava, detects that something reported is inconsistent with the data, the claim is flagged and sent to a human reviewer. Other insurance companies are following suit and turning to AI to expedite claims.

It's evident that *Metromile* collects a large amount of data which makes it necessary to use an enormous number of algorithms and automation to service their insurance policies. However, when it comes to the issue of human involvement, it's much easier for them because they began using machines rather than people. They did not have a large department or team that lost their jobs because of automation. It was not necessary to change the way the company operated. This gives companies like *Metromile* a considerable advantage over existing businesses that often find it difficult to make changes.

So, What Should You Do?

As the world moves to more and more use of automation, choosing to ignore the opportunity will put your company at risk. Competitors or new start-ups will use the technology, and you will not be able to compete. The question is not whether you should use AI, the concern is how to re-engage your labor as you actively employ the new technology.

This might not be as far fetched as it first seems. Think about the agricultural industry. It was only a couple of generations ago that a significant portion of the population was required to provide food. Growing and producing food was labor intensive. Families were large because numerous children were needed to tend to the farm so everyone could eat.

That's not today's reality. Food production is now handled by a tiny percentage of the labor force, yet food can be found in abundance. In 1900, 41% of the workforce was employed in agriculture, but today that percentage is less than two. And even that is going to reduce—thanks to self-driving tractors. These tractors do much more than pull plows, seeders, and harvesting equipment around a field. With greater accuracy in planting systems, seed conservation is increased, and ROI is improved. They can also collect data on soil conditions improving maintenance on already planted crops. This technology allows the farm labor force to concentrate on activity that requires a human touch.

In some cases, part of the workforce can be reskilled, but there will also be cases where some skills would be completely useless. A good illustration of this change is to look at the value of a horse. Not that long ago, horses were necessary for labor and transportation. Today, there is very little work for horses. They are still utilized on ranches but when was the last time you needed a horse for transportation? You can take a horse-drawn carriage around the city perhaps, but it's only for nostalgic reasons. Horses have not disappeared, but they have little work to do.

Transportation is moving toward driverless vehicles. As we noted in the first chapter of this book, work is already being done to create driverless trucks to carry freight across the country. Driverless cars will dominate, not because they are perfect but because they are safer and cheaper.

Very few industries will remain unaffected by AI as we move into the future. Every line of work, even creative occupations will be impacted in some way. Many jobs will be lost; some estimates are as high one third within the next 12 years. All of this will take place as machines make us more and more efficient and productive. The conundrum is that making your company better might require fewer jobs and losing employees. What are they going to do?

Some advocate the idea of a universal basic income (UBI) so that everyone gets money for necessities without doing any work. The concept has been around for a long time, but with the availability of AI and the potential loss of jobs, it has become a serious topic of discussion and debate. There have even been a few experimental programs in various parts of the world. A version has been done in Alaska for many years as the state takes money generated from oil reserves and provides money for residents each year.

On a national level, essentially, the government would provide a set amount of money to each person that would deliver income security. For example, a popular suggestion is $1,000 per month for every adult. Many advocates claim the result will be an explosion in creativity, entre-preneurship, and research. It is also seen as a means for distributing the wealth created by technological advance-ments to more people. This has become a highly charged political issue and points to the fact that some changes will be necessary as AI-enabled robots become more and more productive in the next few years. It is going to change the economic system for many. The question is what is the best way for that to happen.

As your business transitions into AI technology, you need to consider how all of your employees will be affect-ed. You want employees who are enthused by the changes and eager to be a part of the new things happening.[3] If guaranteed basic income comes to pass, you won't have much to worry about since your essential needs will be provided. However, there is a Plan B in case it does not become a reality.

Automation First

While it is essential to spend time dealing with the manpower that is freed up due to automation, it would be prudent not to make the problem even more significant. If you are deciding between starting a new AI function with-in your business or hiring more people, spend the bulk of your time looking at automation as your first option.

There are many automation alternatives already avail-able, with more and more coming online every day. See if the function you are considering hiring employees to do

3   For an interesting discussion about AI and Guaranteed Basic Income see - https://www.quora.com/Will-we-have-a-ba-sic-income-in-the-future

can be better done with automation. If it can, then give it serious consideration. Not only will it help with inefficiencies and saving money, but it will also help avoid a situation where you are likely to end up with even more redundant labor down the road.

As you move into automation, think in terms of retraining whenever possible. Current jobs might not be necessary in the future, but hopefully, your business will expand, and you will need employees in new areas of work.

If you could time travel to fifty years in the past and attend a labor union meeting of workers in the manufacturing industry, you would likely chuckle about the concerns expressed. Probably you would hear someone proclaim, "If you think a machine can take over my job, you don't understand what I do."

If you responded to that union worker's boast and told him what it was like in the future, the entire room would burst into roaring laughter. Describing to them how people will be sitting in front of a bright, lit up screen tapping buttons to do work and earn money, they might have locked you up for being out of your mind.

According to the US Bureau of Labor Statistics, the nation's workforce increased roughly six-fold during the 20th century. In 1900, 24 million were in the workforce of those aged ten and above reporting a gainful occupation. At the end of that century, 1999, the total age 16 and over was 139 million. We've already noted the considerable change in the agricultural industry. Likewise, the percentage working in goods-producing industries (i.e., mining, manufacturing, construction, etc.), decreased from 31% to

19% of the workforce. Imagine giving these numbers to a combined total of 69% of the workforce who were working on farms and goods-producing jobs. How would they react? What would they say?

During that same time period, service industries employment jumped from 31% of all workers in 1900 to 78% in 1999. Many new jobs were created and per capita income increased from $4,200 (time adjusted value) in 1900 to $33,700 in 1999. Even while automation took over some jobs, overall, people and the economy flourished.

The current automation wave forces us to rethink about what humans do better than machines. This list will not include anything that involves routine activities like manufacturing, warehouse distribution, office administration, and even food preparation. Jobs that are generally considered boring and repetitive are most in danger, including moving stuff around, reading documents, and entering data. Humans excel at creative work and deeper thinking.

Back to the Retail Example

Returning to the example that began this chapter and my hopes of working with a major retail company, I still think about what should have happened. The team leader was protecting jobs for the people she cared about, but her thinking was limited. She should have welcomed the change in a minor form at first, using it for a small, confined piece of work and run an experiment.

The results from this experience could then be shared with the team to highlight what the new algorithm did better and where it lacked. A portion of the team could then be assigned to focus on making it work even better. This would have freed up others to put their effort into finding ways to make their stores better than what currently exists in the market.

They would begin to see new opportunities not available before because they were focused on merely keeping the lights on. The companies that are taking this approach are coming up with innovative ideas. For example, a smart mirror placed in a dressing room can suggest items that can be paired with what they are trying on or perhaps shoes that will compliment the outfit. *Amazon's* experimental retail store has shelves with sensors. They track items placed in a shopper's bag and charge it to their account automatically when they leave the store.

Other stores provide iPads for floor staff to better serve customers. They can quickly access inventory, identify complementary products, and even make online purchases with a single click. Other stores are using robots to communicate with customers about how to find an item or send different messages. The purpose is to provide better customer service and sell more products.

In the past few years, the retailer I tried to work with had to shut down hundreds of stores. I don't claim that using our technology would have kept that from happening or that I could have helped them avoid this problem. The truth is we don't know. Also, we'll never know because they failed to see the possibilities.

Chapter 12:

AI as a Department

As I sat down to write this chapter, my first thought was to search *LinkedIn* for people with the job title of "Chief AI Officer." I wanted to get an idea of how many companies have created such a position. The search result came up with 158 people. For all the talk about AI taking away jobs, we can take some comfort in that fact that it has also created at least 158 new jobs. There is some movement toward developing teams with the responsibility of AI. Occasionally, word spreads about an insurance giant or an online marketplace hiring someone from *Google* or *Amazon* as their Chief AI. The movement is beginning.

There is also an entire discussion built around the analogy that "every office that gets water in taps should not hire a chief plumbing officer." I do agree with that thought. However, the thing about plumbing is that you don't change it every day or even once a quarter. Few companies have goals for waste disposal on the agenda for the quarterly planning meetings.

So, who is right—the companies that have Chief AI Officers or the ones that advocate not having one?

Let's Draw a Parallel

A helpful method to find the answer to a question that is new to your experience is to identify a correlation with something familiar and similar but not necessarily related. It helps to take your thinking to an abstract level without sweating the small stuff. So, let's try to do that to answer this question from my personal experience.

I have built and grown a company from two people to a few hundred employees. I have clear recollections of the time I WAS the Chief Plumbing Officer. When there was a water problem in our makeshift office, everyone knew who to call – 1-800-AMIT. It was on everyone's speed dial for all sorts of issues, including plumbing. When necessary, I was more than happy to break out my wrench and other tools and fix the situation.

I was also the Chief Financial Officer, Chief Sales Officer, Head of Engineering, Chief Marketing Officer, and Chief HR Officer. It wasn't quite a one-man show but almost. It was the reversal of the old adage, "too many chiefs and not enough Indians." Look, I'm not minimizing any of these roles. Each was very important. In fact, hiring, making sure everyone was being paid on time, and getting new customers was all I did during the initial years of my startup. However, we couldn't afford to have a separate "Chief" for each of these roles because our scale was tiny. As we grew, the first thing that began to break was financial management. As we added more employees, I found myself sitting beside the scanner for hours during weekends taking care of all the expenses and invoices.

It soon became a ridiculous waste of my time, and I outsourced it to an accountant. He came in once a week and logged all our expenses. As the company grew, this person stepped it up to three times a week until we eventually hired an accounting person as a full-time employee. The same story repeated itself when we opened our first overseas office.

Currently, we have offices in five countries across the globe, and I have an accountant looking into each one. But there is one person I go to when I need to know what is happening across the board. (Thanks Nan, I do not know where I would be without you!) This person has the overall financial picture for all our offices and employees and customers. I would be lost without her, and a lot of people would not get paid on time. In fact, we wouldn't even be collecting money from our customers on time without her.

In addition to operational problems, it was also a struggle to determine if we could afford to make new investments. When I wanted to invest in R&D or lease a new 30,000 sq. ft. office space, I talked to Nan about the finances. She offered her opinion and all the data I needed to make a good decision. Sometimes we run cash flow simulations and play out what-if scenarios on her models to see what might happen in the future. She is a valuable help in maintaining the overall financial health of our business.

The answer about whether you need a Chief AI Officer is hidden in this story from my experience. There are many scenarios where having a Chief AI Officer might not be the right thing if you are still a small business. For example, a transportation company with a fleet of 50 trucks might not need an AI Chief. Certainly, they can benefit from AI, but not the role. Creating such a position makes sense in the following situations:

1. You have a medium or large-scale company
2. There are too many departments – all trying to make sense of AI
3. There is a great deal of redundant use of AI from one department to another

A Chief AI Officer can help you think through the overall AI plan. It is her responsibility to tell you what can and cannot be done, to run what-if scenarios, and roll out AI prototypes to make sure you have a clear picture of what is happening all across your company with AI.

Think about other Chief Officers currently in your company. What and how much do they do for you? What would happen if they were not around? Do they provide strategic firepower to differentiate your business? An AI Officer is no different. She would be just as effective provided you have enough work for her.

Another Perspective

Have you noticed the difference in experience when you go to a museum or visit a place of interest with and without a guide? You miss out on a lot of interesting observations, facts/figures, and background stories without a guide. A guide can improve your experience enormously. There is a phone app called Gypsy Guide created for just that purpose. Simply start driving, and the virtual tour guide will point out things of interest along the way using your phone's GPS location. It's much more informative than trying to find stuff on your own. The following review of the app was recently posted:

"We did the road to Hana on June 18, 2018, and the Gypsy Guide was awesome. We had done the trip 11 years earlier and there was no comparison. It gives a lot of very relevant advice based on where you are and also helps plan ahead by laying out choices down the road and helps pick where to stop and what to skip based on how early in the day it is. On the ride back you get a very interesting history of Maui that makes the long ride back actually enjoyable."

This might be an accurate description of your AI journey. You can try to figure it out on your own, and you might have some success, but you're likely to miss out on a great deal of relevant advice as well as wasting time planning. You will find that it's helpful to know what to skip and where to invest. A Chief AI Officer can be that guide.

Chief AI Officer – Business Person or Technologist?

Once the determination is made to hire a Chief AI Officer (CAIO) for your company, the next step is to determine if you want a technologist or a business person. They will bring a different perspective to every problem and question. My experience is as a technologist for the better part of two decades of my professional life. Also, I've managed both, an exceptionally outstanding team of technologists and business people.

I've witnessed a couple of rare instances where good technologists graduate on to become equally good business people. I caution that these are rare instances.

The ideal CAIO should be a business person with a good grasp of technology and AI. She must be comfortable building and managing a team of AI technologists and can harness their skills, energy, and focus to solve business problems. Since AI technology is new, it's easy to lose focus by trying to do too many things at once. Every new advancement or open source framework is a potential distraction that can cost hours and sway you away from delivering technology that can make a difference for your business. With a business person at the helm of all your AI initiatives, you can be confident that business value will come faster.

Compared to most other CXOs in your company, the CAIO has an additional hurdle to overcome—turning skeptics and non-believers into believers. No fancy presentation or any amount of talking will overcome this hurdle. It's only possible by incrementally but consistently delivering business value through AI. The business value might be in terms of reducing costs or increasing sales or creating competitive advantages. Measurable results will help the CAIO turn your entire team, partners, and customers into AI believers.

When to Hire a CAIO – Do you need one to start?

This depends on how well you understand AI and your own personal belief. If you are confident about what

AI can do for you and where to start, then you should start building your AI Department, beginning with the CAIO.

However, if your still a little skeptical or don't understand the complete context of what AI can do for you or where it can help, then reverse the process and hire from the bottom up. Hire an AI Manager or a Technology Manager with a strong background in AI and build a small team around this person. Allow the team to run some experiments or little bets for you. Give them one specific problem to solve and make sure you have a quantifiable way of measuring the success or failure of this experiment.

If they are successful, provide more tasks in an unrelated area to determine if they can add value across all your business functions. For example, if the first test focused on finance, make the next on marketing or sales. When you begin to see success in multiple areas, then it is time to hire a CAIO. Task them with redesigning your business with AI as the centerpiece.

The CAIO Job Description

Obviously, the job description for your new CAIO must be consistent with other members of the management team. Job descriptions typically span a few paragraphs and often contain bulleted lists of what is expected of the employee. CAIO should focus on the following three Key Performance Indicators (KPI) for your business:

- Save Money
- Save Time
- Improve Competitive Advantage

An excellent place to start when it comes to saving money is with the largest spending department in the company with low-level skills. The average salary and the total spend in the department usually give you a good idea for your starting point. For example, you may be spending 2.5 million dollars in salaries for the engineering department and 2 million dollars in your warehouse salaries. At the outset, it looks like the engineering department is the right place for you to start. But when you look at the data in more detail, you figure out that you have 25 engineers making an average of $100,000 a year, but you have 50 warehouse people making $40,000 a year.

A lower average salary indicates positions that may not require highly skilled employees. The engineers cost the company $2.5 million, and the warehouse workers cost $2 million. The average salary tells you that lower-skilled warehouse jobs might be ripe for automation. Other companies will identify jobs like data entry operators or fleet drivers. This information can be used by the CAIO to run little bets and show some tangible benefits and how AI can impact your bottom line.

The same approach can be used to determine how AI can save time as well as money. The CAIO identifies the part of the business that spends the most time and then looks for ways that AI technology can help reduce this time. For a legal firm, this might be wading through piles of contracts, emails, and other documents. For a retailer, it might involve writing product descriptions before they are listed on the website. Just as you would with money saving options, run a small experiment to test your conclusions. This will allow the small bets to produce tangible benefits before you fire the big guns.

Improving competitive advantage can be more challenging than saving money or time. The CAIO will need to interact with your customers to understand what they value most and what would make your company better than anything else that exists in the market. It might also require an analysis of what your competitors are doing as well as interviewing industry analysts to see where the industry is heading. Compiling all of this information can once again reveal opportunities to produce little bets to run as experiments to see if you're on the right track.

One warning—do not look at technology first and see where it can be used. This is tantamount to looking for nails because you're holding a hammer. Looking for a place to use what you already have will distract you from realizing any tangible business benefits.

Set Your CAIO Up for Success, Not Failure

Don't be surprised that for a period of time, AI is more overhead than bottom line contributor. Like most investments, it takes some time before becoming profitable. You will face the temptation to cut back or reduce spending before it has time to produce results. That's understandable, and I've been there and done that myself.

Another warning is to make sure you set aside enough money and resources to make your AI venture successful. If you are constrained by the budget, take smaller AI steps until you can line up the necessary funding. A CAIO by himself is not going to be successful. At the very least, it requires the following:

1. Data Scientists
2. Computer Vision or NLP Specialists
3. Machine Learning Engineers
4. Application Developers and Testers
5. Data Generation Team

This list is ordered in decreasing order of salaries you will need for these roles. The absence of this essential support team will cause your CAIO to be unsuccessful.

AI As a Department

Once you begin utilizing AI to redesign your business, you will see that it can cut across departments very quickly. Your HR department, marketing, sales, logistics, legal, etc.—all of them can benefit from AI. The same way all departments go to HR for hiring or personnel-related matters and to the finance team for all accounting queries, they should start to come to the AI department for all of their AI needs.

This centralized team will help you get a cross-sectional view of your business and re-use skills and technologies. Take a minute and think about how you decide if you need a department of... anything.

Fundamentally, departmentalizing is an organizational technique for achieving economies of specialization. Companies organize departments based on purpose, location, or customers. The issue of whether to establish

AI as a department in your company should be settled by the same rules that you use already to decide when you need a department. If AI is going to be a small piece of work for your company to begin with, then you can roll it up under your CTO or CIO office. If you are a technology company and AI is at the heart of your distinction, then you should create a dedicated department for this work.

Coming Back to 158

After looking for Chief AI officers on *LinkedIn*, I did the same search for jobs, and it showed zero search results. If companies are not hiring Chief AI Officers, then where are these guys coming from? This brings out another important aspect of this discussion. As of this writing, there aren't a lot of people who have played the role of Chief AI Officer for a long time. So, posting a job may not be the best way to go about it. Like I said at the beginning of this chapter, most large companies looking for these people are directly approaching people working for *Google, Amazon, Facebook*, etc.—companies that have a head start in AI.

Your CAIO might not come from a direct market hiring. Perhaps you need to seek for someone from these head start companies or get someone who has worked in the AI field but does not have a leadership title today.

Your business and this person can grow together in your AI transformation journey.

Chapter 13:

A New Definition of Intellectual Property

One of the more fascinating aspects of sports is that athletes continually get stronger, faster, and better. They frequently do things that stun the rest of us and create a moment that is remembered for a long time. Such an event occurred in 2002 during a Soccer World Cup qualifying match between England and Greece. A young footballer for England who later became one of the most famous athletes of all time was David Beckham, and that game featured the moment that inspired his celebrity status.

Down by a goal in the final minutes of the game, England needed a win or a tie to advance to the finals. Like all seminal moments in sports history, circumstances arranged the moment that no soccer fan would ever forget. England was awarded a free kick from 30 yards in front of the goal. Beckham lined up to take the kick and the world watched.

His powerful right leg impacted the ball in a manner that caused it to spin and take an unusual trajectory toward the goal. The path of the ball curved like a banana and settled into the goal just out of reach of the goalkeeper. Not only did his teammates embrace Beckham on the field, but the watching world embraced him as well. Today if you ask a soccer fan about something called a "banana kick," they will point to this game and this specific kick.

However, Beckham was not the player who invented the curved football shot, nor even the first to use it in a game. That credit belongs to Manuel Francisco dos Santos of Brazil. Better known by his nickname Garrincha ("little bird"), is considered one of the greatest players in the history of football (American soccer). Along with his more famous Pele, Garrincha led Brazil to the pinnacle of the sport for many years.

Playing in the World Cup in 1962 ironically against England, Garrincha received the ball just outside the penalty area. After pausing for a brief second, he took a shot and sent the ball on the trajectory now known as the "banana shot." In the next round of the tournament, Garrincha scored two goals as they defeated Chile. A headline in the Chilean newspaper read, "What planet is Garrincha from?"

In the days since Garrincha and Beckham, many players have developed the ability to curl or bend the ball. The magical shot has become a more common occurrence in today's game. I'm not a soccer expert, but from what I have seen, I'm sure it takes a tremendous amount of hard work to master this kick. No doubt, it takes years of practice and countless hours of learning different techniques. It doesn't appear to be easy for anyone to replicate.

There is another game that is far more ancient than soccer. Origins of the Chinese game of Go are traced to 2,500 to 4,000 years ago. Many say it's the oldest game still played in the original form. It's basically a board game played on a 9x9 square with black and white stones representing yin and yang. The game migrated from China into Korea and later to Japan where it carries a prestigious reputation.

A system that allowed for professional Go players and an annual tournament was created in 1978. For many years, Japan dominated the competition, but in more recent years, Chinese players have proven to be equal to the challenge. Go was brought to America by Chinese who worked on the Transcontinental Railroad in the 1880s but was not picked up by other cultures. A group of German mathematicians discovered it in the early 1900s, and the *American Go Association* was created in 1937, which today has over 2,000 members.

When you think of complex board games, Chess is probably at the top of your list. However, Go might even be a more difficult challenge. It requires intuition along with creative and strategic thinking. There has been speculation for a long time about how difficult it would be for AI to solve.

Before 2015, the best AI programs only managed to reach amateur levels in the game. Experts predicted that AI was still a decade away from achieving a win against a top Go professional player. However, in 2016, *Google* DeepMind developed *AlphaGo* and scheduled a five-game tournament against Lee Sedol, an 18-time world champion Go player. *AlphaGo* was victorious in four of the five games.

The most significant difference between *AlphaGo* and previous AI efforts is the way it applies neural networks that learn the game itself rather than relying on information programmed by humans. This new technology is also being applied to many other areas that use AI.

However, my purpose in relating this event is not to praise AI and *AlphaGo*, but to reference a move made by Lee Sedol in the one game in which he defeated *Alpha-Go*. On the 78th move, Sedol did something unexpected which obviously threw *AlphaGo* off and turned the game in his favor. The move was referred to as something divine and became known as the "God Move."

This amazing board game move by Sedol compares with the banana kick of Garrincha. Both required years of work before adding it to their armory. Players don't worry about the movement being "copied," because it can't be copied. To utilize this weapon requires years of work and practice. It's not possible to simply watch the move and then say, "I'm going to start doing that!" It requires tedious work in addition to mastery of the game's fundamentals.

AI changes all of that.

Since losing that match, *AlphaGo* will probably never lose to that same move again. It will decode the reasoning and logic for the move into its own learning network by running millions of iterations across a wide array of computing resources at its disposal. In other words, it will learn the move very quickly. One of the fundamental features of all AI systems is the ability to divide a massive task into smaller tasks and run them at the same time in parallel on numerous machines. It can then assemble the results.

This capability allows AI to compress time.

Previously, something that would have taken as much as 100 hours of work can now be done in less than one as long as there are more than 100 computer instances available to participate together in computation. In other words, it's not going to take years to perfect a banana kick or the God move. It's a simple matter of doing years of work in parallel.

Does that mean all these players should not work hard to protect their intellectual property by forbidding AI systems to learn from their data without explicit permission?

As an AI specialist, if I put together a learning engine for chess and feed it all the games that Gary Kasporav has played in his life, does the AI engine's knowledge of chess belong to Gary or me? Who owns the Intellectual Property (IP)?

In the age of AI, IP has assumed an entirely new meaning. In the past, if we perceived someone taking a long time or finding it extremely difficult to replicate something, we concluded it does not need to be protected as IP.

I spend time working with young entrepreneurs and advising startups. I recently encountered an exciting startup that has worked on a solution that eliminates the need for physical ID cards, like the ones used in offices to enter the building. I had heard about this startup about six months ago when they began work on implementing their idea, but they were not open to discussing their product in detail.

However, after our recent meeting, I realized the reason for hesitation. Although their idea is exceptionally innovative, it's not that difficult to implement. They spent six months filing a patent application to protect their IP so now they are comfortable discussing the details.

This is important because our approach to IP in the past has rested on the principle of unique things that are not difficult for others to replicate. Now, with AI, many things that we thought were difficult to replicate, are easy. We need to put serious thought into protecting stuff that is produced as a result of our intellectual labor. Intellectual and emotional intelligence is one area where we do not see AI taking over humans in the near future, but we must learn to protect our IP and what it means in the new world.

Chapter 14:

My AI vs. Your AI

AI is not a magic elixir that will automatically make your company better than your competitors. For a moment, let's assume you and I have competing businesses, selling tax planning software to mid-market manufacturing companies. Our products are similar. Yours has an excellent forecasting module, mine provides performance insights based on historical and industry data. Our hit rate for closing sales deals is approximately 15%--we convert 15 prospects into customers for every 100 that we communicate with. It's a tight, competitive market.

Both of us are working to improve our Return on Investment (ROI) on our sales spending. The desire is for our sales team to focus on customers with the highest probability of closing. We have both heard about the promise of AI and are eager to see if it will help us get higher than a 15% rate.

A large Customer Relationship Management (CRM) tool in the market has announced they recently released the AI-enabled version of their tool. It promises to increase sales ROI for every user. We both give it a try to see if it works and makes sense. Unknown to each other, we both sign up to use the new tool. Now, both of us are using the same AI system to help us improve our business.

The question now is, will my AI be better than yours? Or, will it be the same as the capability of the CRM tool?

The simple answer is no. One AI will not be better than the other. The only reason it might work for one and not the other is if one sales team does not use it properly. If they fail to log all the required data, don't use it to full capacity, and make other mistakes, they will lag behind. For comparison sake, let's assume we are both astute managers and lazy teams are not a problem for either of us.

If every company is using AI, what have we achieved by adopting it for ourselves? It might make us a little better, but not remarkably better than competitors in the industry. Any of my competitors that can afford the tool can have the same level of AI as my company.

The Role of Data

Fundamentally, AI depends on data for learning, and it only presents what it learns from the data it receives. An AI engine that has never seen good data will never provide meaningful information.

Let me highlight this with two stories.

About a year ago, I was asked if it will ever be possible for an AI to have a psychedelic trip. If I didn't know that it had already happened, I would have dismissed the question as flippant. It occurred with Norman, MIT's psychopath AI Bot. In 2015, the question was posed concerning the danger of runaway data and the possibility of learning bias caused by source data. Within a year, a test was developed to determine if AI can not only detect but also induce extreme emotions in humans. The goal was to learn if machines can learn to scare us.

The AI was named the Nightmare Machine and it produced psychedelic patterns that were somewhat disturbing. Researcher Pinar Yanardag Delul explained, "We use state-of-the-art deep learning algorithms to learn what haunted houses, ghost towns, or toxic cities look like. The algorithm extracts elements—such as a bruised-black palette—from these scary templates and implants them in the landmarks."[4] The result is abstract photos that may or may not be scary.

I'm confident that the only difference between Norman learning good stuff or bad stuff is the data. Providing data for AI is like the upbringing for a child. You can raise a financial genius or a monster depending on the information you provide for it to learn. A few years ago, a *Twitter* bot named Tay, identified as an experiment in "conversational understanding," was set loose on an innocent AI chatbot. Tay, developed by Microsoft, gets smarter and smarter as it learns to engage in casual and playful conversation.

However, it didn't stay that way long. Via *Twitter*, people sent hateful, misogynistic, and racist comments that Tay picked up and began creating its own comments. An unanswered question is how to teach AI by using public data without incorporating all the bad stuff that comes with human behavior.

---

4   https://www.washingtonpost.com/news/morning-mix/wp/2016/10/24/clinton-trump-the-white-house-too-terrifyingly-transformed-by-mits-nightmare-machine/?utm_term=.92b272b2e59d

When to Use Off the Shelf AI?

Returning to our discussion—subscribing to products that everyone else can use as well, will not give you any significant advantage. It still might be a good thing to do because you gain efficiency but understand your competitor can also become equally efficient. Now, do not get me wrong—there are instances where this might be a totally awesome idea.

The key to making this decision is to look at business functions that create differentiation for your customer. I run a technology business, our Unique Selling Point (USP) is the algorithms we use to make sense of data. Financial accounting is an integral part of my business, but we do not create competitive differentiation for our customers because of our accounting—that responsibility rests with our tech team.

I will not hesitate to use an external financial product that uses AI to help us manage our cash flow better. But I will not let an external engine come close to our tech. This situation might be entirely different for an accounting firm. Their USP is likely to be their financial processes. So, they should be happy to use other tech that uses AI but not let anything come close to their financial processes.

To summarize, it's okay to use an off the shelf AI product for business processes that are not differentiating for your customers. But for your USP, you should get the AI product to come to you, sit with your data and make sense of it—for you and you only. Harvesting the real opportunity that AI presents can help you put miles between you and your competition. The key to this harvest is data—your data.

Data is the New IP

I wrote an article on *LinkedIn* two years ago with the title, "Data is the new IP." Some people also use the expression that "Data is the new Oil." It's necessary to understand how profoundly data affects your AI.

Imagine you are Danny Ocean planning your next heist with the Ocean's 11 team. You have figured out a way to take over a building and hold it for ransom. You have narrowed down your search for an ideal venue for the heist–DreamVille. The sleepy but wealthy town of DreamVille houses headquarters of a large national bank, a few casinos, a bullion retailer's secured warehouse, and a data center of a large company.

Which building do you pick to hold for ransom?

If you chose the casino or the gold warehouse, you should think again. The most valuable asset of a city is its data center. More valuable than a bank and far more precious than bars of gold–data centers house invaluable assets for businesses—their data.

Traditionally, IP has been thought of as an algorithm or process or a way of doing something. It has always been logic driven. Examples are the way *Apple*'s Airpods connect with its phone or how software compresses and distributes data as it is stored in a magnetic medium.

But the changing world of AI will force us to think of data as IP. It will be a fundamental, irreplaceable resource that can differentiate the quality or effectiveness of one AI from another. Having dealt with numerous customers in the context of AI and Machine Learning, it has become apparent to me that the quality or accuracy of a company's AI or Machine Learning algorithms is mostly a factor of the data they have to train and learn. The same algorithm can produce average quality of prediction or accuracy when trained with different data sets. It's not the technology but the data that is the new IP.

Google discovered this truth earlier than most. They give away high-quality services like emails, messaging, and social media for free to everyone in exchange for data. This is not to suggest that their technology is trivial—on the contrary, it is quite superior. But, with all due respect, it is not impossible for others to build it. What others do not have is access to their data. That makes them better than most.

In fact, a few years ago Microsoft launched their search engine called "Bing" in order to grab a market share of the online ad market. I would wager that Microsoft's technology was not dramatically inferior to *Google's*. But they did not have access to *Google's* data to train their algorithms to improve relevance. They have been accused of stealing data from *Google* to bump up their search relevance.

Google ran a sting operation that they claim proved their point. *Google* noticed that Microsoft's competing search engine, Bing, was repeating results that were remarkably similar to *Google* results. They felt the statistical pattern was too indistinguishable to ignore, so they created a test to prove their theory. Nonsensical search queries were created and entered into the search box on *Google's* homepage. Within a couple of weeks, the nonsensical queries began to show up in Bing searches.

What these two computer giants are fighting over is data. The question is whether it is illegal or just clever. *Google* saw it as cheating. A *Google* spokesman said, "I don't know how else to call it but plain and simple cheating. Another analogy is that it's like running a marathon and carrying someone else on your back, who jumps off just before the finish line."[5] This episode reveals the importance of data to two of the largest companies in the world.

As you start planning your AI journey, it is of utmost importance for you to know that though some AI will have extremely unique algorithms and approaches but what will differentiate most of them will be the availability of data for extracting intelligence. If you take away only one thing from this book, let this be it. Understand the value of your data and the role that it will play in uniquely positioning your business in the future.

Let me leave you with a little known story about AI at work. In 2007, *Google* launched a telephone directory listing service called GOOG-411. It was designed to be an alternative to dialing 411 on your phone and provided speech-recognition software to search a directory and place a call to the desired number.

The service was only in operation for a few years and completely shut down toward the end of 2010. The explanation for closing down is fascinating. In an interview, Marisa Mayer, the then VP of Search Products and User Experience explained, "You may have heard about our [directory assistance] 1-800-GOOG-411 service. Whether or not free-411 is a profitable business unto itself is yet to be seen. I myself am somewhat skeptical. The reason we really did it is because we need to build a great speech-

5   https://jamessiminoff.com/post/3055091130/i-dont-know-how-else-to-call-it-but-plain-and

to-text model... that we can use for all kinds of different things, including video search."

Mayer continued, "The speech recognition experts that we have say: If you want us to build a really robust speech model, we need a lot of phonemes, which is a syllable as spoken by a particular voice with a particular intonation. So we need a lot of people talking, saying things so that we can ultimately train off of that... So 1-800-GOOG-411 is about that: Getting a bunch of different speech samples so that when you call up or we're trying to get the voice out of video, we can do it with high accuracy."[6]

Google Home, their AI assistant that you can use in your home, is one of the best speech recognition engines in the market today. The likely reason is that it had an enormous amount of data to use for training. *Google* has a long history of building great products and giving to users for free to grab their data. The data that *Google* does have access to is used to create products and then offered to you for free to learn from your data.

I have a *Google* home device that I keep disconnected. I get the feeling that it uses me more than I use it.

Your Activity

The following is a small snapshot of one section in *Google's* privacy policy on what kind of activity they track when you use their products:

"We collect information about your activity in our services, which we use to do things like recommend a You-

---

6   http://blogoscoped.com/archive/2007-12-17-n30.html

Tube video you might like. The activity information we collect may include:

- Terms you search for
- Videos you watch
- Views and interactions with content and ads
- Voice and audio information when you use audio features
- Purchase activity
- People with whom you communicate or share content
- Activity on third-party sites and apps that use our services
- Chrome browsing history you've synced with your *Google* Account

If you use our services to make and receive calls or send and receive messages, we may collect telephony log information like your phone number, calling-party number, receiving-party number, forwarding numbers, time and date of calls and messages, duration of calls, routing information, and types of calls."

Any surprises? Did you expect to see Voice and Audio information captured when you use YouTube? Do this quick check now. Open your phone's privacy settings and go to microphone and location access. Take a look at the list of all the apps accessing your phone's microphone and location that have no reason to do it. A lot of apps and companies are building their ocean of data collection by sucking your data without explicit consent.

Here is a fascinating read on all the data that *Google* collects from you: https://policies.*Google*.com/privacy.

Google realized before any of us that data is the new IP and they have built a treasure trove that every other company will need a lifetime to catch up to. Now, I don't want to take anything away from *Google*—they have outstanding engineering talent. But the thing is, a company like Microsoft may succeed in luring some top engineering talent from *Google*, but it will never have access to the data that you and I gladly gave to *Google*.

I am confident that their AI will be top of the line in part because of their engineering talent but also because of the data that it has access to. When you draw your AI strategy, be a *Google*! In fact, I want you to promise me that you will take extra care of your data. Go ahead and make that commitment. Put the book down, fire up your email, and send me an email with the subject - "I will be a *Google*" to ainabled@*Infrrd*.ai.

Draw a line in the sand to treat your data with more respect and care by sending me this email.

Do it now.

Chapter 15:

Magic Unfolding

Like many rapidly growing companies in today's world, Alpine Inc. is unlike some of the past giant companies. They don't conduct meetings in dark paneled conference rooms with everyone sitting around a large mahogany table in plush chairs. On most days, their executives and team leaders are busy executing plans made at the beginning of the quarter, ensuring that tasks are accomplished, and goals met.

Today is a date that has been marked on everyone's calendar for months—the quarterly planning meeting. This is the time when all the company leadership gathers in a conference room of a nearby resort. Half the time is spent relaxing around casual activities and building team unity. The other half consists of a quarterly planning meeting. The schedule begins with a look back at the just-completed quarter. This time is crucial because it helps them understand what did and did not work. They will discover some actions to avoid in the future as well as celebrate the successful strategies. When the meeting is finished, they will have re-aligned strategies and agreed upon goals that will guide the company for the next three months.

Like all the quarterly meetings, Alex, the founder and CEO of Alpine Inc. will be steering the ship. Alex began this venture 15 years ago after spending several years working for two large technology corporations. At his side is Riya, the Vice President of Human Resources. Riya has been anticipating this meeting because she had a fantastic quarter and met her targets related to hiring and retaining employees. It was a monumental task since the number of employees needed was significant, she came up with the creative solution of purchasing a small company that ramped up the speed of hiring.

Sherry is also in the meeting. She is the newest member of the leadership team and the most unsure of herself. Her title is SVP of Sales, and her team had a challenging quarter. Although it was discouraging for Sherry, it was in line with everyone else's expectations. Historically, this is a slow quarter for the company. Sherry had some new ideas and wanted to break that tradition, but it wasn't a complete success.

To encourage her fellow team member, Riya spoke up to reinforce a point she frequently makes. "It's not us, it's our customers." She went on to explain that customer's budgets are often not approved this early in the year and they're still working out how to spend their money. She assures Sherry it will pick up. "You need to stop fighting this, Sherry" she added.

"I know, I know," demurred Sherry, "but I'm certain we can do something else to make up for this quarter. I'm not giving up. I will get this back on track... so help me God!"

"Amen to that" chimed in Aiden. He is the company's General Counsel and Head of Legal Affairs, and it's a natural part of his personality to encourage people. He loves to hear people who are determined to make things happen.

His words of encouragement were echoed by Judy, the head of the Marketing Department, "You go girl!"

Larry, in charge of company finance, joined the chorus, "Look at you, loud and raucous like kids. I look forward to these offsite times to get away from the noise of my kids, but this is no different."

Everyone knew he was kidding, but Drew, the VP of Logistics and Warehousing spoke up, "I know, right? Where does a man need to go to find some peace and quiet?"

Like a parent, Alex reclaimed control over the meeting. "Settle down everyone. Let's get back to business. Now, before we go any further, did you guys finalize the name?"

They all knew what Alex was talking about.

"Colin," Riya blurted out first.

"Colin is so British," Sherry said. "Xavier has a butler sounding ring to it... Like Jeeves."

C'mon, Ladies! This is superhero stuff. We've got to have a Superhero name. It's got to be Flash," insisted Drew.

Realizing the obvious that there was no consensus, Alex spoke up. "Alright! Enough already! Clearly, there is no decision yet." He continued, "Before others start throwing out the name Catherine or whatever other names you have come up with for our AI engine, I'm making an executive decision and picking the name myself."

"Albus."

Journey Toward Singularity

The term "Singularity" describes a point in time when AI surpasses that of human intelligence. This is not a science fiction invention but the opinion of many thought leaders in the AI world. Massayoshi Son, the richest man in Japan and founder of a giant tech company, understands the potential better than most. He speaks of Singularity being when AI finally exceeds what humans can do, both with intelligence and physically, and replaces an enormous number of jobs.

Speaking at a recent conference, Son suggested that in addition to white collar and blue collar jobs, there will be a metal collar. It will replace most blue collar jobs and many white collar jobs causing us to have to reflect on the value of our lives. He adds that we "have to think once more, deeply."[7] Son's timeline is 30 years in the future, but at that time, every industry will be redefined as the tools become smarter than mankind.

Even though the characters painted in our short stories in the second part of the book are from different companies, running different functions, there is absolutely no reason that they all cannot be part of a single company, working off the same AI engine. Interesting things start to happen when you have a single engine being used for all your AI needs across your company. What the engine

7   https://www.cnbc.com/2017/09/20/masay-oshi-son-warns-of-the-singularity.html

learns from sales can be applied to marketing, what it sees in hiring can be used for engineering planning. When the data for all the functions of the company flow through one engine, that is when the magic unfolds.

Instead of buying and using separate AI-enabled products for different functions of your company, you should aim to get to a single AI system for all your tasks. That is one step in the direction of achieving Singularity.

Chapter 16:

Roadmap for AI Enablement

In Part 1 of the book, I wrote about the roadmap for transforming your business into an AI-enabled enterprise. Roadmaps are strategic plans that we use with many of our customers to help them think through how they should go about making a change. It brings order to chaos and can help clear your thinking about what to do when and in what order. The AI roadmap that I recommend is divided into seven steps.

1. Business Mapping
2. Disruptors Identification
3. Data Planning
4. New Roles for Humans
5. Measure, Learn, Adjust
6. Full Throttle

Let's talk about these phases, one by one.

Phase 1 – Business Mapping

The starting point of your business transformation is to take a fresh look at your entire business to see how it should look in the new world. Which parts will continue to add value, which pieces need to be upgraded, and which ones need to be tossed away entirely. Like our short stories characters, Riya, Judy, Aidan, etc., you need to think about how your business will look in ten years.

Three aspects help you think about this:

- Struggles
- Optimizations
- New Avenues

Struggles

As you map your business, identifying the problems you struggled with in the past and labeled as impossible to solve is an excellent place to start. In a 1962 book, *The Prospect of Immortality*, Robert Ettinger wrote, "Clearly, the freezer is more attractive than the grave, even if one has doubts about the future capabilities of science. With bad luck, the frozen people will simply remain dead, as they would have in the grave. But with good luck, the manifest destiny of science will be realized, and the resuscitees will drink the wine of centuries unborn. The likely prize is so enormous that even slender odds would be worth embracing." That book gave birth to cryonics, the process of freezing the body at death in the hope that scientific advances will restore it to life one day.

While it is true that at extremely cold temperatures, it's possible to preserve dead bodies and avoid deterioration, the assumption that a person can be unfrozen and the fatal disease cured is yet to be accomplished. Essentially what cryogenics hopes to do is delay an unsolvable problem until the time comes that it can be solved.

With AI, many problems that were unsolvable before have now become solvable. A good example is understanding handwritten text. Until recently, automatically understanding handwritten text from documents had a low accuracy rate. This rate accuracy did not justify the cost of automation because the ROI did not work out.

That is no longer true with AI. We have consistently helped many businesses extract data from handwritten documents that were previously judged impossible to read. This was made possible because of the gaps in traditional systems that were filled by AI. As you think about customer dealings in the past, you probably marked out things that were not deemed possible at the time. These problems provide a good starting point to explore if the problem can now be solved. The answer might be a surprise.

All of us have read about flying cars and other vehicles in comic books as a kid. A company called *Jetpack Aviation* is developing something that looks a great deal like a flying motorcycle. It's an example of solving a problem previously thought unsolvable (flying cars). Just because something hasn't been solved doesn't mean that it can't be solved. AI is proving to be a tool capable of such challenges. Use that inspiration to find shelved projects and ideas that can give your business a 10X edge over your competition.

Optimizations

The second bucket of problems that you should look at are ones that are already solved in your business, but you have never been happy about them. These are the problems whose solutions can feel like a complete waste of time and money. It is something that has been solved, but you have said to yourself numerous times, "There's got to be a better way! This is... [stupid, lame, ridiculous - pick your adjective].

At my home, we have two boys who love Legos. Although the toy is excellent for developing creative and inquisitive skills, any parent who has had boxes full of Legos will attest that they are a problem to clean up. This hits hard when you're barefoot early in the morning and step on one. You can't help but think there has to be a better way to pick these up. My kids hate cleaning up Legos because it's a tedious process of picking them up one at a time. Also, some of the pieces are a few centimeters long and difficult to find and pick up. Someday I'm going to crack open our Roomba (automatic vacuum cleaner). I will integrate it with a computer vision algorithm, so it picks up Legos and only Legos.

In your business, it's likely you have problems that you put up with because you are unaware there is a better solution available. These problems are a good candidate to put on your roadmap.

Take a look at *Airbnb*. Their business model requires finding a balance between having available lodging for guests to book while keeping properties occupied frequently enough to make it worth the host's time and effort. The problem is that hosts don't know what to charge, so *Airbnb* developed a price-setting algorithm based on features and location. However, they discovered the algorithm was too rigid. Finally, they developed one of their trademark technologies using predictive analytics that generates the optimal price for any given day. This AI-based system provides fluid suggestions, and it allows hosts to experiment with rates and provide feedback.

This price optimization works because it's able to combine fixed data like the number of beds and bathrooms, location, amenities, etc., and shifting data like season, local events, available inventory in the area, etc. Reviews are also factored into the data. *Airbnb* pricing is one of the company's most popular attractions for travelers, and it also allows hosts to reap benefits, earning an average of $924 per month, nearly three times the income of its nearest competitor.

New Avenues

This is a more complex area because it's not as easy to identify as the others and it requires creativity. New Avenues refers to graduation opportunities for your business that can help you move up the value chain and create new revenue streams. At the beginning of each quarter, I ask our Executive Team to ask themselves, "What else should we be doing that we are not doing today?" This is one of the more difficult conversations that we have each quarter because it's hard to answer. For executives, who are deeply absorbed in running the day to day operations of their department, it is a challenge to abstract out and think about stuff that we are not doing today.

After numerous failed attempts at getting something meaningful from my executive team, I decided that they need to stop thinking about their business in order to get their creative juices flowing. If they think about ideas related to their business, they're programmed to reflect on what, how, and who of the ideas and nothing kills an unborn idea quicker than logistics. Therefore, we try to pick up industries we have nothing to do with and then draw a parallel to our business.

For example, we might begin the conversation by discussing the flying motorcycle and the kind of problems it solves, or perhaps self-driving tractors and what that means for the agriculture industry. From there, we try to figure out what might be the flying motorcycle for our business, or what would be the self-driving tractor for our customers. These discussions typically helps get creativity flowing.

TV network *CBS* is working with *Nielson* on something called addressable advertising. The term describes ad messages that are addressed to individual viewers. For example, it will allow car advertisers to target viewers who are currently car shopping or have a certain level of income or other traits. The use of smart TVs has made an enormous amount of data available to content providers and advertisers are able to target more specialized audiences.

You need to figure out a way to see what new avenues are now available to your business. What else does AI enable you to do that can put you years ahead of your competition.

Once you have thought through and debated the three dimensions of Struggles, Optimizations, and New Avenues, you have completed the first phase of your AI enablement.

Phase 2 – Identify Disruptors

Sometimes you have ideas about how to change your business to evolve, and at other times the ideas are forced upon you. This usually happens because a new disruptor has attacked your market and changed the rules of how the game is played. *Netflix* is a prime example of a disruptor for traditional cable networks, *Dollar Shave Club* disrupted *Gillette's* long-running shaving business, *Uber* disrupted the taxi business globally. When a disruptor enters your market, you have no choice but to evolve.

When *Teska* jumped into the auto business, they completely changed the industry. They first released "Autopilot" in 2015, not for the purpose of making a self-driving car, but to keep the vehicle from veering out of its lane. Other car manufacturers have followed with a similar feature in their high-end vehicles. *Teska* also set off a significant movement toward electric cars and analysts now predict by 2040, more than half the cars on the planet with be electric. Of course, other car makers are following suit. Perhaps the most threatening feature *Teska* offers is updating software and producing vehicles that are capable of learning. That makes cars from other companies vulnerable to obsolescence.

Akshay Anand, an analyst for *Kelly Blue Book* recently described *Teska's* impact on the industry. "I think the most critical thing that *Teska's* done in terms of the rest of the automotive industry is create a greater sense of urgency as far as innovation and electric. I don't think you would see as many car companies putting all these chips in the electric basket and doing it with a sense of urgency."[8]

It's crucial that you continually review what's happening in your industry. Attend an industry conference to discover companies that evoke the following reactions from you as you see them:

- "That's funny."
- "Those guys are never going to make it."
- "Are you kidding me?"
- "It's a nice experiment, but you can't make a business out of that."

Airbnb, *Facebook*, *Uber*, *Netflix*, and *Google* have received these same reactions earlier in their lives. Try to abstract yourself out of your business and think about what you would do if your worst assumptions about these companies were to come true. That will help you think through what you should experiment with in phase 5.

Phase 3 – Data Planning

Whatever AI initiative you decide to pursue in your roadmap, you will need an abundance of data to train your algorithms. Depending on what you are trying to accomplish, you might land in one of these three states for your data readiness:

1. I have it.
2. I do not have it, someone else does, I can get it.

---

8   https://www.businessinsider.com/*Teska*s-influence-on-the-auto-industry-2018-

3. I do not have it, no one else seems to have it either.

Let's deal with these situations.

The first one warrants no discussion. You need data for training your algorithms, you already have it, all is well, so move on to more exciting things.

For the second state, where you do not have access to data, but you know someone else who might be willing to share with you, you need to figure out a deal or a partnership. If the other party has the rights to sell data and is willing to do it, then it is a matter of negotiating a deal structure that works for you.

If you cannot find anyone in your circle who has this data, then you should also pay a quick visit to www.figure-eight.com. This company tags, annotates, and provides data for training needs. If you can source your data from them, then you are good to go.

The last state is the trickiest one—you do not have any data and you do not know anyone who has it, even the folks at *Figure Eight*. What do you do? You will need to pull a GOOG-411, my friend. Remember how I told you in an earlier chapter that when *Google* needed voice data for training its algorithms, it provided a 411 service for a few years and collected a wide variety of data. Where I live in the bay area, I often see *Google's* self-driving cars being ridden by engineers with open laptops, trying to collect data on teaching the vehicle how to navigate traffic.

This could potentially be a costly proposition—depending on the size of your business, you may or may not be able to afford it. Which brings us to an interesting point. What do you do when you know you cannot have access to the needed data? In some selective cases, AI can come to your rescue and help you create data for your training needs. But for most others, you should stop going any further until you get access to the data. The answer to your data need lies in the three steps mentioned above. Find it before you move forward.

Phase 4: New Role for Humans

This is not necessarily a problem that must be solved as a part of your roadmap but solving this can dramatically improve the chances of your success, and it is the right thing to do for your employees. As described in Chapter 11, when you fund a development which may create job redundancies, you may experience resistance from people who are trying to do the right thing by their friends and colleagues.

You can help everyone by spending time in exploring what role your current workforce will play in the automated world. In most cases, you will notice that AI will make your workforce better—more efficient, productive, or smarter. For example, if your drivers start using AI-based navigation to help them plan their routes, then they will become more efficient. In some cases, they will be thrilled to discover paths that they did not think were possible. If that is the case, then you do not have a problem.

Otherwise, you will need a plan to re-engage your workforce in alternate roles as suggested in Chapter 11.

Phase 5 – Little Bets

This is where the fun starts. You are now ready to make little bets to validate your AI idea. This would be something that you get to assign a small budget to confirm your AI hypothesis. For instance, if you run a nationwide property maintenance service and you want to figure out which lawns are not maintained well, or which houses have the biggest lawns that you can pitch to, then your little bet would be to have an AI algorithm estimate the size of a yard from satellite imagery. Or it might be rating on a scale of 1 to 10, how well a lawn is maintained.

The little bets mode precedes full solution phase. The purpose is to validate one or two critical pieces that AI must deliver for it to make business sense. A little bet can be a short-term experiment, perhaps three to six months. A more complex solution might require a year or more. At this stage, it can be done in-house or by finding a technology partner to assist with these bets.

Phase 6 – Measure, Learn, Adjust

The purpose of this phase is to learn from your little bets to determine if AI can deliver what you need and if it's possible to build a business case. Return to the lawn mowing company referenced earlier. Your little bet might reveal that it is possible to estimate the size of the lawn from satellite imagery, but the measurement is only accurate 70% of the time. After a few calculations, you determine it will cost $250,000 to run this solution for one year. You realize it can process 40,000 houses' data for each of your 137 regions. If you get a positive ROI, you can move forward. However, you might calculate that the math does not support the ROI unless accuracy is higher than 85%, so it becomes a deal breaker for your company.

Based on your measurements, you attempt a second little bet to see if you can reliably improve the accuracy from 70% to 85%. If your small bet succeeds, then you move on to the final stage.

Phase 7 – Full Throttle

Now that you have concrete data and math to support your AI investment, you can go full throttle and accelerate the AI enablement. At this point, it is no longer an experiment, it has become an operational unit whose cost will need to be measured, budgeted, and return on capital calculated like any other business unit. You will also put together a management team to run this unit effectively and connect it with other pieces of your organization like sales, marketing, etc.

Once you complete the first initiative, then you can repeat these seven steps to enable further business initiatives.

Chapter 17:

Infrrd - My Own AI Story

After graduating with an engineering degree, I wanted to start my own business. While in college, I began putting computers together and selling them. Most of my customers were parents of students who wanted to buy computers or small businessmen who needed a basic computer for accounting and bookkeeping. Selling to businesses was easier than selling to individuals. This experience taught me that I should focus on selling to businesses.

After graduating, I took a job with *IBM* where I worked for over six years. Most of that time was spent at one of their facilities in the Washington DC area. I worked for another large consulting firm for another five years after leaving *IBM*. During this time, I worked on solving the toughest technology problems for customers. If anyone said "this cannot be done," I had to give it a try. More often than not, tinkering led me to solutions that others thought were impossible.

I harbored the idea of starting my own venture for a long time. In July of 2009, my wife and I welcomed our first son into this world. The same guy from the first chapter who wants to be a pilot one day. His birth was a wake-up call for me. I figured as this little guy grows up, he is going to need a lot of time from me. If I had to do something, it had to be done now. When he was 15 days old, I quit my corporate job. That was almost ten years ago. The next eight years of my life were a roller coaster ride filled with scary highs and depressing lows. That journey deserves a book of its own.

We started our business by helping our customers make sense of unstructured data. The kind of data that does not live in structured databases like numbers. Stuff like emails, photos, videos, documents, legal contracts, etc. We did a lot of bespoke development work at that time. Then we started working on our first platform that dealt with Natural Language Processing. This was long before NLP became cool. After trying a few markets, we found a niche in retail.

In my past life, before I started my own venture, I had consulted for some of the largest retailers globally as a lead technology architect. My time there taught me that there is a fundamental difference in the way retailers sell products. Most people tasked with the job of describing products for a retail website have never seen the product in real life and certainly have not had a chance to experience it first hand.

Consequently, they write descriptions that are specification oriented. They write things like, "this shirt has blue checks," "it is 60% cotton, 40% polyester," or "it is also full sleeved and has a button down collar." But this is not how customers look at products. No one goes to *Amazon*.com and searches for 60% polyester blue check shirt.

Customers look for most products based on what they want to use it for or use it with. There are a lot more people who search for "dress for beach wedding" than "red full-length dress." But retailers had no way of knowing which products were good for what situations without trying them out.

We filled this gap by analyzing millions of product reviews that customers left on websites after buying and using a product. Instead of using the technology available at that time, we built our product from scratch to find topics of interest in conversations. The beauty of our algorithms was that they were not programmed with preconceived ideas of what to expect in conversation. I used to compare that with the legal terminology of "leading the witness."

If you have written a product review or answered a survey, you probably know what I am talking about. Usually, these feedback forms give you a list of answers to select from. They had questions like - What did you like about this dress - color, fitting, price. The trouble with this kind of feedback is that the user doesn't have the option to tell you what they honestly feel because you have boxed their universe of feedback to a few options for answers.

Our algorithms read reviews without knowing what to expect in the review. If enough people were talking about something, it would automatically come up in our analysis. The results that we found blew me away.

Here are a few memorable ones that I remember:

- **Dresses for the Mother of the Bride**

We analyzed numerous reviews for a retail customer and discovered that many mothers were talking about wearing a dress to their daughter's wedding. Think about that for a second. Can a dress manufacturer or designer tell you that they have designed this dress specifically for the mother of the bride? No. Only a mother who has used the dress for that purpose can provide this insight. Once we made this discovery, we also saw this was a popular search term on *Google*. It meant that a lot of people were searching for dresses for the mother of the bride. We helped our customers connect with these shoppers and make a sale.

- **Baby Food Blender**

When it comes to blenders, your first thought is probably making smoothies or juices. While that's true, our analysis also revealed that many mothers are using blenders to make baby food. It makes sense because it allows parents to be in control of what they feed their children. However, we also discovered that not all blenders are good for making baby food. A few types were given obvious preference by mothers. This was a great marketing opportunity for our customers.

- **Perfume for Interviews**

This one caught me off guard. When our NLP highlighted this discovery, I was sure there was a bug in our algorithm. But, it turns out that when people go for interviews, they don't want to smell too strong. The preference is for a subtle, milder smelling fragrance that is not distracting for the interviewer. Apparently, searching "perfume for an interview" is a thing and neither our customer nor we had the slightest idea.

Armed with this new capability, we helped many retailers better understand what they were selling and increase their revenues. Our typical customer usually realized a 15-40% increase in revenue from product discovery.

Over the next few years, we added computer vision capabilities to our platform. This allowed us to describe a retail product by just looking at its picture. We could tell you that this was a dress with a crew neck and floral prints, with a distressed look and something that customers would love to wear during the summer.

Then a few years ago, some customers approached us to pull out similar insights from financial documents. These documents had some fairly complicated tables and charts that contained insights that needed to be extracted automatically. We began by using the same algorithms that we used for extracting insights from reviews to extracting insights from financial documents. But here is the kicker—our computer vision algorithms that we used to analyze photos of dresses also helped us analyze photos of tables and graphs. We were able to extract data that most other companies could not.

Since then, *Infrrd* has helped numerous financial services and manufacturing companies bring AI into their business for automation. There are a few important lessons that I have learned through this journey, and I want to share them through this book.

1. Don't Take my Data, Bring Your Algorithms

In the not so distant future, with extensive work being carried out by algorithms, data is going to be the only true differentiator. At a high level, AI is made up of algorithms and data. You can hire awesome engineers to build amazing AI algorithms. When it comes to data—you can either follow Nielsen's approach of sending out mailers promising a few bucks for a completed survey or *Google's* strategy of giving away free software and apps that capture data. However you choose to get your data is up to you but you cannot steal your competitor's data.

In Chapter 14, I quoted the following statement by Marissa Mayer speaking about how they used *Google*-411 to accumulate data: "The speech recognition experts that we have say: If you want us to build a really robust speech model, we need a lot of phonemes, which is a syllable as spoken by a particular voice with a particular intonation. So we need a lot of people talking, saying things so that we can ultimately train off of that."

Google's speech recognition engineers needed data for training, so they created and offered a free service for a few years to gather that data! That is the level of obsession you need to show with your data. When you get an external company to provide your AI solution, ask them to bring their algorithms to your data. Do not send them your data. The next few years will give rise to a whole new Data Economy, make sure you are on the right side.

Remember: One company's AI can only be better than another's because of the access to the data it has.

2. The World's Best Things are Custom Made

Which product do you think *Facebook* used to build *Facebook*?

How about *Google*? Which search engine did they use to build *Google* search?

Which eCommerce product does *Amazon* use to run its store?

The answer is none.

They have all built tailored solutions for their business. If you want a cheaper version of an eCommerce website, you can get one up and running for a few dollars a month. But it will not be as innovative, disruptive, or scalable as *Amazon*. Interesting frameworks or products come out of what these companies make, but commercial products are not the centerpiece of their own systems.

Productization is a big thing in the world of technology. It refers to the acts of modifying something, for example, a concept or a tool, in a way that makes it usable as a commercial product. It's probable that you've heard of *WordPress*. If you read blogs or view websites, then you have utilized their product. It has been described as "a factory that makes web pages." It is a product created by modifying a concept to make it usable and useful for others.

Products help you scale your business since it allows you to onboard a lot of customers without any significant change in your engineering costs. They have economies of scale built into their model. For AI solutions, this perception needs to change a little bit. Because even though two given companies use the same AI model, for instance, a mortgage application, there are nuances in how their people have dealt with the data in the past. You can get amazing results by customizing 15-20% of your AI solution against these nuances. So do not look at customization as a bad thing for AI. In fact, I would encourage you to go as custom as you can to get solutions that no one has access to.

All the examples that I have cited in this book–from *Airbnb's* pricing algorithm to *Google's* speech recognition are all custom made solutions for them.

3. AI is Not Just Another Technology

Ten years from now, when we look back at companies that did not survive the AI disruption wave, we will find that many of them looked at AI as just another technology. AI is far more than that. It's a fundamental shift in how businesses are run. A lot of work that is done by humans today will be transferred to machines. Each executive will need to re-design their business and put people to work in opportunities that did not exist before. Make sure you keep an eye on that and do not ignore this opportunity to transform and avoid the disruption.

4. IP Has a Whole New Meaning Now

Because of the ease with which AI learns, we should treat every intellectual or sports move as potential Intellectual Property (IP). IP should not only be focused on stuff that others can copy easily but also on intellectual by-products. The 1889 commissioner of the US Patent Office, Charles Duell had allegedly said, "Everything that can be invented has been invented." He thought that the patent office would not last long and will shrink in size quite a bit after the initial rush of inventions dies down. If he did say that, then he could not have been more wrong.

Not only has the world invented a ton of IP since then but it is about to take a whole new meaning. Imagine a chess player filing for a patent for his new move that he developed or a sports person trying to patent a new shot that he conjured after years of practice and refinement.

You may also see disclaimers before live sports game that warn you that all the moves that you are about to see in the game are the intellectual property of the players. And they should not be reproduced or replicated without explicit consent of the player. I would wager that the time is not too far ahead before this becomes a reality.

The same will become true for businesses as well. You need to start looking at your data and the data of your customers in a new light and try to ascertain the intellectual value embedded in it.

5. Workforce Redundancy is Imminent, and Hope is Not a Plan

By one estimate, there are more than 3.5 million truck drivers in the US. Do they know what is coming? Should they be worried? As more and more jobs are taken over by machines, we will have an increasing pool of redundant workforce.

Just in the past few months, news reports have made this change something experienced by people today, not in the future. *PepsiCo* informed workers in Texas and New York that they will be laid off in a few months. They are cutting positions that will be automated as they are relentlessly working to streamline and automate their processes.

State Street, a leader in the investment world has announced plans to lay off nearly 1,500 works in a move to automate services. Only 10% of those jobs involve senior management so the majority affect less skilled positions. We frequently hear about the loss of jobs in the auto industry. Many factors impact this workforce segment including foreign competition, trade tariffs, labor costs, and many others. However, auto manufacturing has also been greatly affected by automation, and it will continue to spread making an impact on the workforce.

As an executive in an enterprise, you will need to plan this out. The best thing you can do for yourself, your business, and the person you are about to hire is to see if this is a job that needs sufficient intellectual capital to be relevant through automation. If you are not convinced, then you should look for automation solutions and not hire that person.

6. Central AI Would Be a Big Thing

Numerous companies have AI solutions for specific areas—AI for chat, AI for this, and AI for that, but this is all very counterintuitive to the idea of the intelligence. Think about the science fiction movies or TV series you have seen. Whenever they talk about the future, there is always ONE computer or brain that controls the whole thing. Star Trek does not have one computer controlling all the doors and another one for navigation and yet another one for communication. The promise of all Sci-Fi entertainment has been ONE central AI system.

Now, I realize it's fiction, but think about it in the context of your business. It makes perfect sense to have one AI system with fundamental capabilities that can be used across the board. You will be far ahead if you work on that and not start a collection of unrelated, disconnected AI, and consequently, ineffective AI.

Glück!

All the stories in this book are inspired by our experience with our own customers. These were innovative companies looking for AI-based solutions to help them become more efficient. The company that they all stumble upon in these chapters was *Infrrd*. We have enjoyed putting solutions together that our customers didn't realize were possible. Along the way, we have created a lot of AI believers and AI-nabled a lot of businesses.

I hope you found something of value in this book and I wish you all the best with your AI Enablement journey.